IN
AMERICAN
HISTORY

THE CUBAN MISSILE CRISIS IN AMERICAN HISTORY

Paul Brubaker

Enslow Publishers, Inc.

40 Industrial Road   PO Box 38
Box 398   Aldershot
Berkeley Heights, NJ 07922   Hants GU12 6BP
USA   UK

http://www.enslow.com

Copyright © 2001 by Paul Brubaker

Library of Congress Cataloging-in-Publication Data

Brubaker, Paul.
    The Cuban Missile Crisis in American history / Paul Brubaker.
        p. cm.—(In American history)
    Includes bibliographical references and index.
    ISBN 0-7660-1414-2
    1. Cuban Missile Crisis, 1962—Juvenile literature. I. Title. II. Series.
E841.B75   2001
973.922—dc21

                                      00-009663

Printed in the United States of America

10 9 8 7 6 5 4 3 2

To Our Readers: We have done our best to make sure all Internet addresses in
this book were active and appropriate when we went to press. However, the
author and the publisher have no control over and assume no liability for the
material available on those Internet sites or on other Web sites they may link to.
Any comments or suggestions can be sent by e-mail to comments@enslow.com or
to the address on the back cover.

Illustration Credits: Archive Photos, p. 34; Enslow Publishers, Inc.,
p. 29; The John F. Kennedy Library, pp. 6, 11, 40, 42, 48, 51, 54, 55,
63, 66, 72, 73, 80, 83, 88, 107; Library of Congress, pp. 20, 36;
National Archives, p. 16; Sagamore Hill National Historic Site, p. 25.

Cover Illustration: The John F. Kennedy Library.

★ CONTENTS ★

WHAT WAS EVERYONE SO AFRAID OF?

He had a boy about the same age as [my son] John," said President John F. Kennedy, upon hearing the bad news that Major Rudolph Anderson, Jr., a United States pilot, had been killed.[1] Anderson's U-2 surveillance plane was struck by a Soviet surface-to-air missile (SAM) as he was flying over Cuba just after ten o'clock that morning.

It was Saturday, October 27, 1962. Thirteen days earlier, Anderson was one of two pilots who brought back the first photographic evidence of Soviet nuclear missiles aimed at the United States on the island of Cuba, ninety miles away from Florida. The discovery had started the conflict known as the Cuban Missile Crisis—the first time that the United States faced the threat of a nuclear attack.

Anderson's aircraft, the U-2, was capable of taking clear photographs of the ground from very high altitudes, but it carried no weapons. As he was gathering information about Soviet activities in the nearby island nation, his U-2 was spotted by a Soviet radar station

President Kennedy (right) and his brother Robert, the attorney general, deep in thought outside the White House.

in Cuba and shot down. President Kennedy remarked to his brother Robert, the United States attorney general, "it is always the brave and the best who die." He knew the tragedy of Anderson's death would be overshadowed by what it meant to the worsening crisis.[2]

"How can we send anymore U-2 pilots into this area tomorrow unless we take out all of the SAM sites?" the president asked. He was considering a massive attack against the Soviet forces in Cuba, but realized, "We are in an entirely new ball game."[3]

Up to this point, Kennedy had wanted to avoid using military force, even though many of his advisors did not agree. In fact, when the crisis first began, the opinion of the "ExCom" (short for executive committee—the president's advisors during the crisis) was that the president should send bombers into Cuba to destroy the Soviet missiles.[4] President Kennedy believed the United States should avoid any action that could start a war with the Soviet Union. Instead, he wanted to find a diplomatic way to persuade the leader of the Soviet Union, General Secretary Nikita Khrushchev, to remove the missiles from Cuba. The death of Major Anderson, however, had heightened the crisis. Military action had become necessary. Four days earlier, the president had promised the ExCom that United States fighter planes would immediately fly to Cuba and destroy a SAM site if a U-2 were fired upon.[5]

Later that afternoon, President Kennedy reconsidered that promise. His Joint Chiefs of Staff (heads of the branches of the military) and the ExCom wanted him to send bombers to Cuba the next day. They also wanted to destroy the nuclear missile bases by Monday. The president wanted to delay the use of military force a little while longer. He had Secretary of Defense Robert McNamara tell the ExCom that he intended to send more surveillance aircraft, instead of bombers, into Cuba in the morning.[6]

The news of Anderson's death had raised some questions with the president. He wondered if the firing of the Soviet SAM that killed Anderson had been an accident. It was possible that Khrushchev may not have given the order to shoot down Anderson's plane.

Perhaps a Soviet soldier in Cuba had fired on the U-2 out of nervousness, fear, or a simple misunderstanding of his orders. If so, then Kennedy was risking a world war over a mistake.

False Alarms

President Kennedy had good reason to be cautious. Since the crisis had begun there had been other incidents that nearly triggered nuclear war between the United States and the Soviet Union. On October 25, 1962, B-52s—long-range heavy bombers carrying nuclear weapons—were nearly dispatched from Volk Air Field in Wisconsin with orders to attack the Soviet Union. The bombers were responding to their command center in Duluth, Minnesota, which was being invaded by what was believed to be a Soviet spy. The "spy" ended up being a wild bear trying to break the fences around the base. Volk Field was so small that it had no air tower. Trucks had to rush out onto the airstrip to keep the B-52s from taking off and attacking the Soviet Union.[7]

Another incident happened the following day. A radar station in Moorestown, New Jersey, noticed a missile off the coast of Florida. The missile's origin had to be determined quickly. It was estimated that it would only take ten minutes for a missile to travel from Cuba to Washington, D.C. The missile veered out into the Atlantic Ocean. It was found out later that it had been an American missile launched from Patrick Air Force Base in Florida—part of a routine test. This was an extremely close call. If any Soviet radar station had seen the same missile, Soviet officials might have thought it was an attack on the Soviet Union and fired their own missiles at the United States.[8]

On the same day that Anderson's U-2 had been shot down, President Kennedy received the news that another U-2 had become lost and had accidentally flown over the Soviet Union. The plane had taken off from Alaska. It was assigned to take air samples to find evidence of nuclear testing on the eastern end of Russia. After Soviet fighter planes tried to intercept the U-2, American planes, armed with nuclear warheads, had also taken off. Fortunately, the U-2 eventually found its way back to Alaska, and hostilities were avoided.[9] Clearly, the Cuban Missile Crisis was a situation in which even the smallest mistake could have had devastating consequences.

Kennedy wanted to be absolutely certain of the Soviet Union's intentions as he responded to the attack on Major Anderson's U-2. Therefore, he decided to send more U-2s to fly over Cuba the next morning. If the Soviets fired at them, he would know the Soviet Union was planning to go to war. This would also delay a military offensive and give Kennedy one more night to find a peaceful solution to the Cuban Missile Crisis. After the last ExCom meeting of the afternoon, President Kennedy had his brother Attorney General Robert Kennedy arrange a secret meeting with the Soviet ambassador in Washington, D.C.

A Secret Meeting

Few meetings have been as important as the one held between United States Attorney General Robert F. Kennedy and Soviet Ambassador Anatoly Dobrynin. The two men met alone. In fact, most of the members of the ExCom were not even aware that the meeting was taking place.

Robert Kennedy brought a simple message for Dobrynin to send to Khrushchev. Unless the Soviet Union removed the missiles from Cuba by the next day, the United States would take military action to remove them. In fact, United States forces could do this within two hours of the president's order.[10] Although Robert Kennedy understood that the Soviet Union might fight back, he said the end result would be "not only dead Americans but dead Russians as well."[11]

"I've never seen him like this before," said Dobrynin in his message to Khrushchev. "[Robert] Kennedy was very upset . . . [he] persistently returned to one topic: time is of the essence and we shouldn't miss this chance. . . . After meeting with me he immediately went to see the president. . . ."[12]

By the end of that Saturday night, President Kennedy was not happy. The message Robert Kennedy had brought to Dobrynin was sent to Khrushchev in Moscow at 9:00 P.M. The State Department, which is in charge of the United States' relationships with other countries, sent memos to the American ambassadors working in allied nations. The memos said that time

A public demonstration took place in front of the White House during the Cuban Missile Crisis. Those on the far side of the street wanted the United States to invade Cuba. Those on the near side wanted a peaceful solution.

was running out. The United States might have to use military force to remove the threat of the Soviet missiles in Cuba. Bombers were ready to attack if the U-2s were fired upon during their morning flights. In addition, fourteen thousand men were ready to invade Cuba, if necessary. All hope rested with the Soviet leader's changing his course of action within a few short hours. President Kennedy expected that war with the Soviet Union might begin as early as the next day.[13]

Earlier that day, two groups of people had been marching outside the White House. On one side of the street, people held signs that said, "Invade." They wanted the president to use military force to solve the problem of the Soviet missiles in Cuba. On the other side of the street, people carried signs encouraging peace. Outside the White House, the American public was clearly demonstrating President Kennedy's two choices in the Cuban Missile Crisis.

THE COLD WAR

The United States and the Soviet Union, for much of the twentieth century, were engaged in a conflict known as the Cold War. This term was first used by journalist Walter Lippmann to describe the unique relationship between the two superpowers. (A superpower is a nation that dominates world affairs because of its military strength.) The Cold War had no actual fighting between the enemies. In fact, if fighting ever began between the two nations, it was likely that the consequences would be devastating. Therefore, in order to avoid war, both nations tried to exert their influence by gathering allies all over the world. This could be described as a "turf war." The result was a world divided among nations that were friendly with either the United States or the Soviet Union.

The superpowers also tried to intimidate each other through the arms race. This was an aspect of the Cold War in which each superpower tried to make or possess more destructive weapons than the other. Behind the turf war and the arms race was the basic difference between the United States and the Soviet Union, which may have been the biggest cause of the

Cold War. That difference was in the idea upon which each nation was founded.

The War of Ideas

Each superpower had a different idea of how the world should be. The American Declaration of Independence said that freedom for each individual person to have "life, liberty, and the pursuit of happiness" was most important. The United States' economic system of capitalism fit naturally with this idea. In capitalism, a person can start a business and compete in a free market in which only the best businesses survive.

Vladimir Lenin, the leader of the Russian Revolution of 1917, disagreed. He believed in the ideas of Karl Marx, a German philosopher who hated capitalism. Marx said that capitalism led to the abuse of the largest group of the world's population—the workers. During the Industrial Revolution, in which many nations switched from farming economies to factory-based economies, there were many business owners who made huge profits off the labor of people who were grossly underpaid and subjected to harsh working conditions. The result was that a few people grew wealthy from the labor done by people who barely made enough to survive. To Lenin, communism (a system in which the government owns all the businesses and distributes a nation's wealth among the people) was the solution. Lenin also believed in Marx's prediction that working-class people all over the world would one day rise up against those who owned businesses.

This idea of a worldwide revolution is what made the United States very fearful of the Soviet Union.

World War II Starts the Turf War

Although the United States and the Soviet Union would become tense Cold War enemies, the two nations put aside their differences when they needed to conquer a common enemy. During World War II (1939–1945), the two nations joined with Great Britain, France, and others to form the Allied Powers against Nazi Germany, Italy, and Japan—the Axis Powers. Differences in beliefs were put aside in order to defeat the Axis.

As it became more likely that they would win the war, the Allies had to plan how the world would be after World War II. Many of the decisions made during World War II would later have significance in the Cold War. The Soviet Union (USSR) gained a huge amount of land at the Yalta Conference in 1945. Decisions made there allowed the USSR to influence the governments of Eastern Europe. Soviet leader Joseph Stalin ruled these countries, as well as the Soviet Union, with absolute power. British Prime Minister Winston Churchill would later describe Stalin's Communist influence as an "iron curtain" that descended across Eastern Europe. It was as if there were an invisible barrier that separated the Communist nations from the free nations of Europe.

Problems between the superpowers began with decisions that were made about what would be done

The Big Three—British Prime Minister Winston Churchill, United States President Franklin Roosevelt, and Soviet Premier Joseph Stalin—met at Yalta to discuss the organization of the postwar world.

with defeated Nazi Germany and its capital, Berlin. At the Potsdam Conference of July 1945, the Allies agreed to divide Berlin into four sectors, each to be occupied by a different Allied power. When Joseph Stalin later disagreed with the other Allies' plans to rebuild Germany, he tried to force the other Allies out of Berlin by sealing off the railroads and highways to their sectors of Berlin in 1948. The Allies responded with the Berlin Airlift, a year-long, round-the-clock effort to supply West Berlin with food and fuel. Even though Stalin eventually ended the blockade, the crisis worsened relations between the United States and the Soviet Union.

The Arms Race and the Atomic Bomb

Interestingly, it was at the Potsdam Conference that the arms race was born. President Harry Truman received word that the United States had developed a new weapon that would be used to defeat Japan. The weapon was the atomic bomb.

August 6, 1945, began like any other day for the people of Hiroshima, a medium-sized Japanese city. Farmers worked in their fields, and laborers worked in their factories. Stores opened in the middle of town, and young children played near their homes. Although Japan was a nation at war, the people in this town felt relatively safe, far from the fighting. Even the sight of three United States B-29 planes flying overhead did not cause alarm. Residents had grown accustomed to the patrol flights of their enemy. They were certain that, if the United States were going to attack, there would have been many more bombers in the sky.[1]

Then something terrible happened. In one of the busiest sections of the city, people stopped and watched three parachutes floating down through the sky. Moments later, those people were gone. They were instantly burned away. An atomic bomb was at the end of the three parachutes. It detonated and started a huge firestorm that engulfed the city. In an instant, the city of Hiroshima was destroyed.[2]

Some survivors' accounts told just how quickly the atomic bomb wiped out the city. A fisherman who had been working on a nearby bay said, "I saw suddenly a flash of light. I thought something burned my face. I hid in the boat face down. When I looked up later, Hiroshima was completely burned." Another man said, "The tin roof sidings came swirling into my room and everything was black. Rubble and glass and everything you can think of was blasted into my house."[3]

In the heart of the city, the damage was unlike anything ever seen before. Because few people in the immediate area of the blast had survived, the story of what happened had to be put together by the remains. Anyone who went to Hiroshima after the blast saw the gruesome sight of bodies everywhere. Many were burned beyond recognition. Some people, dead and alive, were trapped beneath the wreckage of houses. Trolleys packed with commuters were stopped in their tracks. Inside were only charred figures, some still holding on to the overhead straps.[4]

Just days after the destruction of Hiroshima, the United States dropped another atomic bomb on Japan. This one devastated the city of Nagasaki, finally forcing Japan to surrender and end the war.

The stories and images of Hiroshima and Nagasaki had an effect on the world that would last long after World War II. For a brief period of time, the United States was the only nation to possess nuclear weapons. That changed in 1949 when the Soviet Union developed its own atomic bomb. Americans could no longer consider themselves safe. Each superpower now had the power to destroy the other. If any hostilities escalated to the point where nuclear weapons would be used, both sides would suffer massive losses.

The Cold War Affects Life at Home

Changes in technology would also affect the arms race. Over time, nuclear arms were no longer dropped from airplanes. They became missiles that carried explosive nuclear devices called warheads. When John F. Kennedy ran for president in 1960, he believed that the Soviet Union had more nuclear missiles than the United States. One of his campaign promises was to correct this problem, which he called the "missile gap."

This idea that the United States was losing the arms race touched the lives of nearly everyone in American society. Schoolchildren learned what to do in a nuclear attack in the same way they learned about fire safety. Some even saw a film that featured a character named Burt the Turtle, who would quickly go into his shell whenever there was trouble. The accompanying song said:

> *There was a turtle by the name of Burt*
> *And Burt the Turtle was very alert*
> *When danger threatened him he never got hurt*
> *He knew just what to do*
> *He'd duck and cover*
> *Duck and cover*[5]

"Duck and cover" was the "stop, drop, and roll" of the atomic age. There were even duck and cover drills in school, similar to fire drills. When a special alarm sounded, students crouched as tightly as possible beneath their desks (just like a turtle in a shell) in order to protect themselves from the firestorm, flying glass, and debris of a nuclear attack.

If an attack happened while they were out of school, the duck and cover rule still applied. The "Burt the Turtle" film showed different scenes of people who suddenly had to duck and cover when they saw the atomic blast. A small boy quickly jumped off of his bike and crouched behind a brick wall when he saw the

The nuclear age caused concern among many Americans. Some even built their own bomb shelters, to try to be prepared in the event of nuclear war.

nuclear flash. A family having a picnic saw the flash and quickly ducked and covered beneath their picnic blanket. The voice on the film instructed,

Sundays, holidays, vacation time . . . we must be ready everyday, all the time to do the right thing if the atomic bomb explodes. Duck and cover: that's the first thing to do.[6]

Fear of atomic bombing also affected life at home. Many homes built in the 1950s were equipped with bomb shelters—underground havens designed to help a family survive a nuclear attack. Housewives were instructed how to stock and prepare foods and take care of their families while hiding out in the bomb shelter. People's lives were overshadowed by the grim possibility that a nuclear weapon could end life as they knew it.

The Cuban Missile Crisis made many people's worst fears a very real, and a very grim, possibility. Everyone wanted to be spared a fate worse than that of the people of Japan.

3

HOW DID CUBA GET IN THE MIDDLE?

Just as it is important to understand how the relationship between the United States and the Soviet Union led to the Cuban Missile Crisis, it is equally important to understand how Cuba's relationship with both superpowers contributed to the outbreak of the crisis. Cuba's location, only ninety miles from the southern tip of Florida, was one of the reasons that the United States felt so threatened when the Soviet Union built missile sites in the island nation. Prior to the Cuban Missile Crisis, the United States had grown accustomed to taking advantage of Cuba's location, as well as Cuba's very profitable exports, including sugar and tropical fruits. Reporter Walter Cronkite said, "We considered it part of the United States practically; just a little country over there that was of no danger to anybody. As a matter of fact, it was a rather important economic asset to the United States."[1]

The Monroe Doctrine

For most of its history, the United States not only served its own interests in Cuba, but also in the rest of

Latin America. In fact, it was as early as 1823 that the United States began to show how possessive it was of the entire Western Hemisphere. In his annual message to Congress, President James Monroe issued the Monroe Doctrine. It stated that it was not the United States' policy to interfere with the affairs of other nations. However, the United States would be forced to act if any European power tried to further colonize any territory in the Western Hemisphere. President

SOURCE DOCUMENT

OUR POLICY IN REGARD TO EUROPE, WHICH WAS ADOPTED AT AN EARLY STAGE OF THE WARS WHICH HAVE SO LONG AGITATED THAT QUARTER OF THE GLOBE, NEVERTHELESS REMAINS THE SAME, WHICH IS, NOT TO INTERFERE IN THE INTERNAL CONCERNS OF ANY OF ITS POWERS; TO CONSIDER THE GOVERNMENT DE FACTO AS THE LEGITIMATE GOVERNMENT FOR US; TO CULTIVATE FRIENDLY RELATIONS WITH IT. . . . BUT IN REGARD TO THOSE CONTINENTS [IN THE AMERICAS] CIRCUMSTANCES ARE EMINENTLY AND CONSPICUOUSLY DIFFERENT. IT IS IMPOSSIBLE THAT THE ALLIED POWERS SHOULD EXTEND THEIR POLITICAL SYSTEM TO ANY PORTION OF EITHER CONTINENT WITHOUT ENDANGERING OUR PEACE AND HAPPINESS; NOR CAN ANYONE BELIEVE THAT OUR SOUTHERN BRETHREN, IF LEFT TO THEMSELVES, WOULD ADOPT IT OF THEIR OWN ACCORD. IT IS EQUALLY IMPOSSIBLE, THEREFORE, THAT WE SHOULD BEHOLD SUCH INTERPOSITION IN ANY FORM WITH INDIFFERENCE.[2]

The Monroe Doctrine declared that the United States had an interest in the affairs of all Western Hemisphere nations.

Monroe did not object to the European nations' keeping the colonies they already possessed. At the time, Great Britain, France, and Spain all had colonies in the Americas. Monroe did make it clear, however, that the United States intended to watch and protect its side of the planet.

One of the biggest champions of the Monroe Doctrine would be President Theodore Roosevelt. He described it as "a long step, toward assuring the universal peace of the world by securing the possibility of permanent peace on this hemisphere."[3]

The United States and Cuba

Prior to becoming president in 1901, Theodore Roosevelt became a nationally known figure in the Spanish-American War of 1898. In this conflict, the United States helped Cuba fight to win its independence from Spain. Theodore Roosevelt led his "Rough Riders" in an attack on San Juan Hill, one of the most famous offensives of the war. When the war ended, Cuba was free from Spain, but became a protectorate of the United States. This meant that Cuba was expected to take advice on economic matters from the United States.

The victories the United States enjoyed on the battlefield were not as significant as the victories it won after the war had ended. Although the United States officially recognized Cuba's independence on April 20, 1898, a new treaty was written on May 22, 1903. It redefined the relationship between the two nations.

This new treaty included what became known as the Platt Amendment. It gave the United States the right to intervene in Cuba's government. It also gave the United States the right to buy or lease land from Cuba in order to build a naval base. At the same time, it forbade Cuba to enter any agreement that would allow another country to establish itself in any part of Cuba "for military or naval purposes." An American naval base was later built at Guantanamo Bay on the southeastern coast of Cuba. It still remains one of the United States Navy's most strategically important locations.[4]

Theodore Roosevelt's presidency significantly impacted the United States' relationship with Latin America. His strong support of the Monroe Doctrine was matched only by his belief in the importance of maintaining a strong navy. This was reflected in one of his most

Theodore Roosevelt helped increase the United States' role in the affairs of Latin American nations.

famous quotations: "There is a homely old adage which runs: 'Speak softly and carry a big stick; you will go far.' If the American nation will speak softly and yet build and keep . . . a thoroughly efficient navy the Monroe Doctrine will go far."[5] The United States Navy would make use of the base at Guantanamo Bay to protect its borders and other national interests.

At the same time, Roosevelt thought the Monroe Doctrine had given a special responsibility to the United States. In a message to Congress, Roosevelt said that, when a foreign nation became "uncivilized" or its actions interfered with American interests, it required the intervention of a more civilized nation. If this happened in the Western Hemisphere, the United States would have to act as an international police power. This idea became known as the Roosevelt Corollary.

Changes in Policy Toward Latin America

Cuba's relationship with the United States changed very little until the presidency of another Roosevelt. In 1934, Franklin Delano Roosevelt reached an agreement with Cuba. It released Cuba from the obligations of the Platt Amendment. Cuba gained back some of the independence it had lost in the old agreement. Cuba only had to allow the United States to keep its naval base at Guantanamo Bay.[6]

This new treaty marked the beginning of the United States' Good Neighbor Policy, which lasted until 1945. During this time, the United States interfered less in the affairs of Cuba and other Latin American nations. The problems of the Great Depression, and later, the need to win World War II, seemed more important to the president than policing the Western Hemisphere.

In the years following World War II, the Western Hemisphere went through notable changes. In 1948, the free nations of the Western Hemisphere formed the Organization of American States (OAS). Its purpose was to promote democracy, economic prosperity, and human rights. Member nations, which included the United States, promised not to interfere with other nations' affairs.

Fulgencio Batista, Dictator of Cuba

Meanwhile, Cuba's political instability led to a takeover by Fulgencio Batista. Batista rose to power through a secret takeover, or coup, in 1952. A brutal dictator, he favored the interests of the United States government, North American businesses, and even organized crime.

In a strange way, the Cold War helped Batista maintain the strength of his government. Soon after coming to power, Batista filed requests with the United States for weapons and other military goods. The United States shipped submachine guns, rifles, grenades, bombs, rocket launchers, and other equipment that was supposed to be used to prevent the spread of communism into the Western Hemisphere. However, United States diplomats and military officers knew that Batista's arsenal was not being used to fight his foreign enemies. Instead, he used it to eliminate anyone who opposed him in Cuba.[7]

Batista gave the United States a good reason to help him stay in power. In exchange for indirect military support, Batista allowed American business investors to make a huge amount of money in Cuba. The island nation bought large quantities of American rice, wheat, and flour, and other products. A shopper in a Cuban store would see names such as Borden, Colgate, Goodyear, and Procter & Gamble just as often as a shopper would in the United States. Batista also made it easy to sell American products by dropping all tariffs (taxes on imports) on products from the United States.[8]

The good fortune Batista provided for Americans added to an economic situation that was already working to the advantage of the United States. The Batista government allowed American businesses to open in Cuba without taxing them.[9] By 1958, the United States had become the world's largest consumer of Cuba's most profitable agricultural resource: sugar.[10] However, Batista allowed American companies to buy most of Cuba's sugar plantations and processing mills. The Cuban people were not profiting from their own biggest resource.

Even Batista grew concerned that he could not afford to lose the United States as a trade partner. He looked for other ways for Cuba to make money. He decided to make Cuba a vacation spot. Cuba is a tropical paradise in the Caribbean Sea. A fifty-five-minute flight from Miami, Florida, to the Cuban capital of Havana would bring Americans to beautiful beaches that were perfect for a vacation. After Batista developed Cuba's tourist industry, people could stay in luxurious hotels, see celebrities such as Frank Sinatra and Elvis Presley perform in nightclubs, and gamble in casinos.

While Americans enjoyed Cuba as a vacation getaway and a place to make money, the Cuban government became very corrupt. United States companies that did business in Cuba often appointed Cubans to their boards of directors. This helped them gain influence over the Cuban government. Furthermore, the thriving

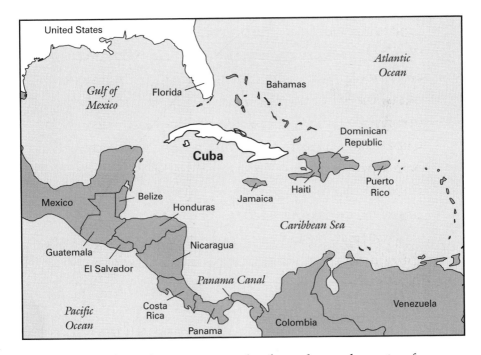

Cuba, located just ninety miles from the southern tip of Florida, was once a place of profit for the United States.

hotels and casinos were often owned by American mobsters, who were able to bribe government officials. Often the decisions made by the Cuban government benefited people outside of Cuba, rather than native Cubans.

The Rise of Fidel Castro

As Batista made a personal fortune selling his government's protection of foreign interests, many of his nation's needs went ignored. "It is hard for a person who comes to Cuba . . . to realize that only a few miles back from the city hundreds of thousands of people have only the bare necessities of life," one ambassador said.[11]

Under Batista's rule, unemployment increased. Many businesses, owned by foreigners, preferred to hire people from their own countries. Other people, like those who worked in the sugar industry, could only work for a few months of the year during the harvesting season. At the same time, Cuba's population was growing. Crimes such as drug selling and prostitution, brought to Cuba with the influence of organized crime, increased.

Batista did nothing about these problems. The Cuban people realized that their leader worked harder to keep foreign powers happy than to solve the problems of his own people. They grew more nationalistic, believing that Cuba should be for Cubans. They wanted to be in control of their own nation, its resources, and its role in the world. Before the 1950s ended, a new leader, Fidel Castro, would come to power with the promise of giving the Cuban people exactly what they wanted.

Fidel Castro had an interesting opportunity early in his life that might have prevented his ever becoming the leader of Cuba. An accomplished baseball player, he was offered a contract to pitch for the New York Giants, an American major-league baseball team. To the team's surprise, Castro turned the offer down to finish law school.[12] By the time Castro rose to power, he had earned four university degrees.

Castro had already decided what was most important to him. He despised the influence of foreign countries that exploited Cuba's resources. He blamed "Yankee Imperialism," as he called the United States' tendency to interfere with the affairs of Latin American countries, for many of Cuba's economic problems. To Castro, Fulgencio Batista was a puppet of the United States, and had to be overthrown.

On July 26, 1953, Castro led a small band of followers in an attack against the dictator. Although they were unsuccessful and Castro had to flee from Cuba, it was the start of Castro's revolutionary movement called M-26-7, or "the July 26th movement."[13]

Castro's exile gave him time to gather followers for his coup. As he talked to anti-Batista Cubans living in other countries, he promised free elections, social reform, schools, housing, and an end to government corruption. In a few years, Castro had gathered enough supporters and money to try again to take over the Cuban government. He secretly returned to Cuba and hid in the Sierra Maestra Mountains. There, he trained his followers to be soldiers, carrying out occasional guerrilla attacks, and waited for the right moment to attack.

The moment came on New Year's Eve, 1958. While most of the wealthy people in Havana were celebrating, members of M-26-7 struck the city and forced Batista to flee the country. The next day, Batista was in the Dominican Republic, a nearby country to the southeast of Cuba. When Castro assumed power in Havana a few days later, the Cuban Revolution was complete.

The United States Reacts to the Cuban Revolution

The world did not know what to expect from Fidel Castro. Some people, including American President Dwight D. Eisenhower, suspected that Castro was a Communist. Some of his behavior made Americans uneasy. Castro executed his political opponents, just as Stalin and other leaders had. Castro defended himself by saying, "What was done at Hiroshima and Nagasaki? In the name of peace two cities were bombed and more than three hundred thousand human beings killed. We have shot no child, we have shot no woman, we have shot no old people."[14]

As people wondered whether Castro was a Communist, the new Cuban dictator angered the United States. In his first year of power, Castro seized

SOURCE DOCUMENT

TO THE ACCUSATION THAT CUBA WANTS TO EXPORT ITS REVOLUTION, WE REPLY: REVOLUTIONS ARE NOT EXPORTED, THEY ARE MADE BY THE PEOPLE. . . .

WHAT CUBA CAN GIVE TO THE PEOPLE, AND HAS ALREADY GIVEN, IS ITS EXAMPLE.

AND WHAT DOES THE CUBAN REVOLUTION TEACH? THAT REVOLUTION IS POSSIBLE, THAT THE PEOPLE CAN MAKE IT, THAT IN THE CONTEMPORARY WORLD THERE ARE NO FORCES CAPABLE OF HALTING THE LIBERATION MOVEMENT OF THE PEOPLES.[15]

Fidel Castro was considered dangerous because of his outspoken support for communism and for revolution around Latin America.

all American-owned businesses and property in Cuba. The United States lost a tremendous amount of money. Castro said he was only correcting a bad situation for Cuba: "The United States was the owner of our electric power plants, of our telephone companies, of the main transportation companies, of the principal industries, of the best lands, of the largest sugar mills."[16]

Then, in February 1960, suspicions that Castro might be a Communist seemed to be confirmed when Cuba and the Soviet Union made a trade agreement. The Soviet Union promised to provide hundreds of millions of dollars in trade and financial assistance to

Fidel Castro looked to the Soviet Union for aid as he tried to create a Communist government in Cuba.

Cuba. The trade agreement allowed Cuba to be free of the United States' economic influence. Cuba would be able to import necessities, such as oil, from the Soviet Union, and would also be able to sell its sugar to the Soviet Union.[17]

The threat of communism so close to home prompted President Eisenhower to take action. He secretly worked with the Central Intelligence Agency (CIA) to attempt to drive Castro out of Cuba or to assassinate him. After those plans failed, Eisenhower and his administration developed a mission to invade Cuba, restore American ownership of seized property, and expel communism from Cuba. Although Eisenhower's administration masterminded the plan, his second term would end before it could be carried out. The invasion of Cuba would be left to the youngest man ever to be elected to the White House, President John F. Kennedy.

4

SOVIET MISSILES IN CUBA

While Eisenhower and the CIA worked on a plan to get Fidel Castro out of Cuba, Senator John F. Kennedy was busy campaigning for the United States presidency. He had plenty of obstacles to overcome.

Kennedy's opponent, Richard M. Nixon, was the current vice president. Nixon had more political experience than Kennedy. Many voters saw Kennedy's youth as a disadvantage. Others were uncomfortable with Kennedy's being a Catholic. They feared that a Catholic president might consult the Pope as he made important decisions that would affect millions of Americans. In order to compensate for his disadvantages, Kennedy attacked the Eisenhower administration, and Nixon's actions within it, for not being strong enough in the face of communism.

"If you can't stand up to Castro, how can you be expected to stand up to [Soviet leader] Khrushchev?" asked Kennedy on October 15, 1960. The young senator criticized Vice President Nixon for describing Batista's government as "stable" when he visited Cuba just before the revolution.[1]

Vice President Richard M. Nixon (left) and Senator John F. Kennedy debated each other on television during the 1960 race for the presidency.

Ultimately, the Kennedy campaign would be successful. He won, by a very narrow margin, the 1960 presidential election. As president, it would be Kennedy's responsibility to stand up to both Castro and Khrushchev.

John F. Kennedy Becomes President

Kennedy's campaign song was "High Hopes," and that was just what he had upon taking the oath of office. Although he was anti-Communist, Kennedy hoped to build better relations with the Soviet Union. While he did not like the situation in Cuba, he understood the part the United States had played in creating the circumstances that led to the Cuban Revolution. He also understood that Fidel Castro, with his charismatic ability to get people to believe in him, intended to spread his revolution throughout the Western Hemisphere. It was up to the new president to uphold the Monroe Doctrine.[2]

Kennedy hoped to stop the spread of communism in Latin America with a program called the Alliance for Progress. In this program, the United States would give economic assistance to Latin American nations to help them "develop the resources of the entire hemisphere, [and] strengthen the forces of democracy." Latin America would share in the benefits of capitalism and democracy, and Kennedy would fight communism without using the military.[3]

These high hopes were met by the harsh reality of what had happened during Eisenhower's presidency. By the time Kennedy was inaugurated in January 1961, President Eisenhower had broken all diplomatic ties with Cuba. This meant that the United States had suspended relations with the nation after Castro ordered most of the Americans working in the United States Embassy to leave Cuba. Trade between the two nations had been drastically reduced. Kennedy inherited these problems, but most importantly, he also inherited Eisenhower's plan to get Castro out of Cuba.

The Plan for the Bay of Pigs Invasion

Eisenhower's top-secret plan was developed by the CIA. It called for using Cuban exiles who had left when Castro came to power as a military force for an invasion of Cuba. The "Exile Brigade" would be trained by the CIA in Guatemala.

Although President Eisenhower approved the CIA's plan on March 17, 1960, an unexpected turn of events complicated the mission.[4] On January 10, 1961, *The New York Times* carried an article reporting on the training of anti-Castro troops in Guatemala. This forced Eisenhower to keep quiet about matters in Cuba. He would have to allow the incoming president to handle the problem. He later wrote in his memoirs:

> So, to the [Kennedy] administration, we left units of Cuban refugees busily training and preparing hopefully for a return to their native land. . . . [T]heir hatred of Castro, their patriotism, and their readiness to sacrifice for the restoration of freedom in Cuba could not be doubted.[5]

President Kennedy Changes the Plan

Kennedy, however, had his doubts about Eisenhower's invasion plan. It called for air strikes to be made at the Bay of Pigs, on Cuba's southern coast. Once that area had been weakened, the Exile Brigade would land on the island. It was expected that its arrival would encourage other anti-Castro Cubans to join the fight to take back Cuba.

What bothered Kennedy was the chance that the world might find out that the United States was behind the invasion. Any aggressive military action might discourage other Latin American nations from joining Kennedy's Alliance for Progress. Kennedy was also concerned about how United States intervention in Cuba would affect relations with the Soviet Union. He feared Khrushchev might respond by taking military action.

Therefore, Kennedy tried to hide the fact that the United States was behind the invasion. Kennedy assured reporters that he did not intend to send United States troops into Cuba. He made no mention of the secret mission that had already been started. Even after the first air strike had been launched and Castro's forces were mobilized in response, Kennedy denied that the United States had anything to do with the attack. In order to keep reporters from getting suspicious, Kennedy made some fateful decisions. He canceled all further bombings and naval reinforcements that the Exile Brigade would depend upon. Finally, the day came when the Exile Brigade would make its landing at the Bay of Pigs.

The mission was an absolute failure. Once the Exile Brigade had reached the Bay of Pigs on April 17, 1961, it was left to fend for itself. Kennedy's reducing the number of air strikes and naval reinforcements allowed Castro's army to cut off the Exile Brigade's supply boats. The helpless group of sixteen hundred Cuban exiles was trapped at the Bay of Pigs. After three days and nights, the abandoned Exile Brigade surrendered to Castro's forces.

The failed Bay of Pigs invasion painfully showed the state of relations among the United States, Cuba, and the Soviet Union. As Castro celebrated the success of his regime, he openly declared that his new government was Communist. Castro and Khrushchev admired each other not only for their likeness in political ideas, but also for their personal similarities. The two had much in common.

Former President Dwight Eisenhower (right) advises President Kennedy after the failed Bay of Pigs invasion.

As the two Communist leaders celebrated their new kinship, President Kennedy dealt with the embarrassment of his first major public failure. He believed he had trusted the experts too much, and that they led him to make some bad decisions. The disaster of the Bay of Pigs invasion made getting Castro and communism out of Cuba a personal issue for President Kennedy.

The Vienna Conference

Relations between the two superpowers were further complicated by the personality clash of Kennedy and Khrushchev. Just a few months after the invasion, Kennedy and Khrushchev met in Vienna, Austria, in June 1961. It was the only time the two men ever met in person. The conference was supposed to improve relations between the two nations. The result, however, was quite the opposite. "The President was completely overwhelmed by the ruthlessness and barbarity of the Russian Chairman," said Harold Macmillan, prime minister of Great Britain at the time. "It reminded me of [someone] trying to hold a conversation with [Adolf] Hitler."[6]

Others at the conference noticed differences between the two leaders. "I had the distinct impression that Khrushchev came to Vienna believing that he was a strong man who had come up in a very tough environment in the Soviet Union," said Kennedy's Assistant Secretary of Defense Paul Nitze. "[He thought] Mr. Kennedy was a rich man's son who had

President Kennedy and Soviet leader Nikita Krushchev met for the first and only time in Vienna, Austria, in 1961.

no such experience." One of Khrushchev's interpreters said, "He took a rather dim view of Kennedy as a President and [he told us] that he pitied the American people that they had a president of that sort."[7]

Khrushchev tried to use the Vienna Conference as an opportunity to take advantage of Kennedy's weakened position after the Bay of Pigs. Trying to succeed where Stalin had failed, the Soviet leader demanded that the United States, along with Great Britain and France, withdraw from their occupation zones in Berlin. Khrushchev had been troubled by the constant fleeing of people from Communist East Germany to capitalist West Berlin. If the former Allies refused to withdraw, Khrushchev would use his military to cut off the entire city from the West. Since Berlin was nestled inside East Germany, an ally of the Soviet Union, Khrushchev could easily carry out his threat.

Despite what Khrushchev thought of him, President Kennedy stood firm. He understood that refusing Khrushchev's demand could start a military conflict. However, giving in to Khrushchev and letting him think that the United States would weaken to appease him could be just as disastrous. In response to Khrushchev's demands, Kennedy said, "Western Europe is vital to our national security. . . . If we were to leave West Berlin, Europe would be abandoned as well. . . . We cannot accept that."[8]

Khrushchev replied, "I want peace, but if you want war, that is your problem."

"It is you, not I, who wants to force a change," said the president. Khrushchev refused to withdraw his demand on Berlin. Kennedy would not give in. The president left the conference saying, "It will be a cold winter." He expected the nations to go to war.[9]

War was avoided, however, by a strange set of circumstances. By order of the East German government, a wall was built to divide West Berlin and East Berlin. The wall was put up to keep people from leaving the Communist East for the democratic West. It was an ugly concrete barrier with barbed wire and armed patrol guards. The wall caused a great deal of heartbreak for the citizens of Berlin, who were suddenly separated from each other. However, it ended the crisis and enabled President Kennedy to concentrate his attention on matters in Cuba.

Mongoose and Anadyr

In the hope of controlling the situation in Cuba, Kennedy authorized a new secret mission called Operation Mongoose. This was a $50 million plan to overthrow Castro in October 1962. During the time leading up to then, six thousand acts of sabotage were committed by the CIA against Castro's government while United States troops were engaged in military exercises throughout the Caribbean Sea.

These events made Fidel Castro nervous. He became certain that the United States wanted him dead or out of Cuba. He expected that attempts would be made against his life and government. He knew his military was not strong enough to defend against United States armed forces. Fearing for his regime, he turned to his best ally for help.

Khrushchev had many reasons to be nervous as well. He, too, felt that the United States would probably try a second invasion. Losing Cuba would make him look like an ineffective leader. The situation in Berlin also threatened Khrushchev. The Berlin Wall had stopped the flow of refugees from his system, but it would not have been necessary to build a wall if he could have forced Kennedy to withdraw from Berlin. Khrushchev also had concerns about his own country's security. Just over the border from the Soviet Union, in Turkey, United States nuclear missiles had been installed since the early 1950s. They were aimed at Moscow.[10]

In May 1962, Khrushchev came up with a way to solve his problems and still avoid war. "I had the idea of installing missiles with nuclear warheads in Cuba without letting the United States find out they were there until it was too late to do anything about them," Khrushchev later wrote. He believed that, in addition to protecting Cuba from the United States, putting missiles in Cuba would help the Soviets equalize the balance of power with the United States.

At the time, the Soviets' intercontinental ballistic missiles (ICBMs) were fewer and not as reliable as those of the United States. (ICBMs are missiles that can be launched from one continent and hit a target on another continent.) Khrushchev liked the idea that missiles in Cuba would "turn the tables" on the United States. He said,

> The Americans had surrounded our country with military bases and threatened us with nuclear weapons, and now they would learn just what it feels like to have enemy missiles pointing at [them]; we'd be doing nothing more than giving them a little of their own medicine.[11]

The plan would be called Operation Anadyr, named after a river on the Pacific tip of Siberia. It was the first step toward the Cuban Missile Crisis.

FINDING OUT ABOUT THE MISSILES

"Whatever happened to the Monroe Doctrine?" asked Homer Capehart, a Republican senator from Indiana. "Never before have we allowed it to be violated." Capehart was using Cuba as a campaign issue against the Democrats in the congressional elections of November 1962. Republicans were characterizing the Kennedy administration as negligent about Soviet activity in Cuba. "How long will the president examine the situation?" Capehart continued, "Until the hundreds of Russian troops will grow into hundreds of thousands?"[1]

Senator Capehart demanded that the United States invade Cuba. His sentiments were echoed by another Republican senator, Kenneth Keating.[2] On August 31, Keating said he had reliable sources that indicated the Soviets had deployed twelve hundred troops to Cuba. He also said there were reports of missile bases being built on the island.[3] Although the accusations that Kennedy had "gone soft" on Castro and communism may have been politically motivated, there was some truth behind the rumors. The Soviets had become more active in Cuba.

Soviet Arms in Cuba

One of the people who was most concerned about Soviet activities was a member of the Kennedy administration, CIA Director John McCone. McCone knew that the Soviets lacked reliable ICBMs. A missile base in Cuba would allow the Soviet Union to launch an attack on the United States using medium-range ballistic missiles (MRBMs), which had a shorter range than ICBMs.[4]

McCone's agency reported to the president on August 22 that an unprecedented amount of Soviet personnel and equipment had recently arrived in Cuba.[5] In fact, during the months of May and June 1962, Cuba had received a variety of defense weapons from the Soviet Union. The CIA had been keeping a close watch on the military buildup. McCone tried to encourage the president to take military action against Cuba. When a U-2 spy flight revealed the presence of Soviet SAMs in Cuba on August 29, McCone knew that any surveillance flight over Cuba would be vulnerable to attack.[6]

Although the president was not considering an attack on Cuba, McCone made Kennedy concerned enough to demand an explanation from Soviet officials. He sent one of his advisors, Ted Sorensen, to meet with Soviet Ambassador Anatoly Dobrynin at the Soviet Embassy in Washington, D.C.

The ambassador was very friendly. He explained that the purpose of the military buildup in Cuba was strictly defensive. He said the United States had nothing

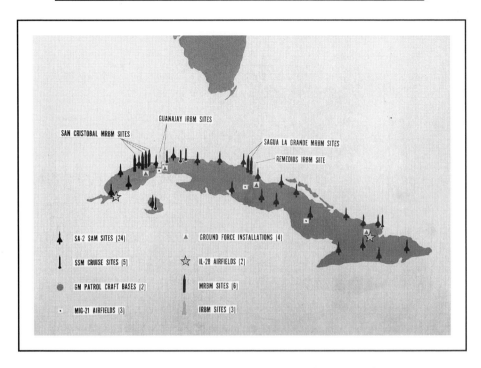

A CIA illustration shows the Soviet military buildup in Cuba in the fall of 1962.

to worry about. He then gave Sorensen a message for President Kennedy from Khrushchev. The message said Khrushchev did not intend to do anything that would "complicate the international situation or aggravate the tension in the relations between our two countries."[7] Indeed, all the weapons that had been detected in Cuba by U-2 surveillance missions up to that point were defensive weapons.

Despite the reassurances that he had received from Soviet officials, the president remained cautious. He ordered forty-five United States warships and ten thousand marines to practice maneuvers just a short distance from Cuba. He also increased U-2 flights over Cuba.[8]

President Kennedy Warns the Soviets

Since it appeared that the United States was in no immediate danger, President Kennedy responded to critics who were dissatisfied with his handling of the Cuba problem. On September 4, he invited fifteen high-ranking congressmen—eight Democrats and seven Republicans—to a meeting to discuss the situation.

At this meeting, he explained that the Soviet buildup in Cuba was only a defensive measure. Even though it was "annoying" to the United States, it was not a violation of the Monroe Doctrine. If anything, he added, Cuba's dependence on the Soviet Union showed just how weak Castro's regime was.[9]

Later that day, the president issued a statement to reassure the American people and also to warn the Soviet Union:

> Information has reached this Government in the last four days from a variety of sources which establishes without doubt that the Soviets have provided the Cuban government with a number of anti-aircraft defensive missiles. . . . [However,] There is no evidence of any organized combat force in Cuba from any Soviet bloc country.[10]

The president then cautioned that, if the Soviets placed any offensive weapons in Cuba, "the gravest of issues would arise."[11] The United States military would be used in Cuba, if necessary.

The president took further action to calm his critics. On September 7, President Kennedy asked Congress to allow him to prepare one hundred fifty thousand troops from the army reserve in case they were needed for an invasion of Cuba. During a press conference on September 13, President Kennedy said the United States was ready to act against the Communists.[12] His tough stance was tempered, however. He reminded the American people that, as long as the Soviet military buildup in Cuba remained defensive and there was no direct threat to the United States, he had no good reason to use military force against Cuba.

The Missiles Are Found

Over the next few weeks, tropical rains loomed over Cuba. The ominous weather prevented American U-2s from keeping watch on Soviet activities on the island. This gave the Soviets the chance to work feverishly on completing launchpads and missiles before the skies cleared. Khrushchev would later describe what he and Castro had done, saying, "We had installed enough missiles to destroy New York, Chicago and other huge industrial cities—let alone a little village like Washington."[13]

By the time surveillance flights could resume, it was October 14. The pilots on the mission were Major Richard Heyser and Major Rudolph Anderson. Once they returned from their mission, the film from the plane's cameras was removed, developed, and sent to a special division of the CIA called the National

Photographic Interpretation Center (NPIC). It was this agency's job to look carefully at the photographs taken by the U-2 in order to determine what had been going on in Cuba. When they examined the photos the day after the U-2's flight, they made a discovery so serious that they immediately sent word to CIA head-quarters in nearby Langley, Virginia.

"Those things we've been worrying about," said a cryptic voice on the phone to Kennedy advisor McGeorge Bundy. "It looks as though we've really got something." Bundy and his wife had been entertaining

MRBM FIELD LAUNCH SITE
SAN CRISTOBAL NO 1
14 OCTOBER 1962

ERECTOR/LAUNCHER EQUIPMENT

TENT AREAS

EQUIPMENT

ERECTOR/LAUNCHER EQUIPMENT

8 MISSILE TRAILERS

CONSTRUCTION

This is the photograph that started the Cuban Missile Crisis, taken from Major Rudolph Anderson's U-2 aircraft.

dinner guests at their home when the phone call, made by CIA Deputy Director Ray Cline, interrupted their evening.

Bundy knew what Cline meant. His first impulse was to call the president. Then he realized that President Kennedy was in New York, campaigning for congressional candidates. He was due back in Washington early the next morning. Bundy made the decision to keep the news to himself. He would let the president have one last quiet night's sleep as preparation for the days ahead. He decided that he would inform President Kennedy of the outbreak of the Cuban Missile Crisis the next day.[14]

At 9:00 A.M. on Tuesday, October 16, 1962, Bundy met with President Kennedy. He brought the news that confirmed the United States' worst fears. The Soviets had been lying about the military buildup in Cuba. Offensive weapons had been installed. American security was threatened. The Cuban Missile Crisis had begun.

President Kennedy was enraged at Khrushchev when McGeorge Bundy gave him the news that there was photographic evidence of missiles in Cuba. He wondered how the leader of the other superpower could be trusted in anything, since he had been lying all along. However, the

KEEPING UP APPEARANCES

president put his anger aside. He immediately concentrated on getting the missiles out of Cuba.

Bundy was instructed to begin more surveillance flights and to gather some of his most trusted advisors for a secret meeting.[1] These advisors were the ExCom. Some of the members of the ExCom would be at every meeting throughout the crisis, helping the president. Others would come and go as they were needed. All were chosen because the president trusted them. Kennedy's bad experience with the Bay of Pigs invasion made him very cautious about taking advice from someone solely because of his or her expertise. However, the ExCom was not lacking in experts. It had members from the State Department, the Defense Department, the CIA, and other top government agencies. The first ExCom meeting took place Tuesday, October 16, at 11:45 A.M.

The ExCom in session with the president.

Appointments, Meetings, and Information Gathering

In the early stages of the Cuban Missile Crisis, keeping the news secret was of utmost importance. If the Soviets knew that the United States had found the missiles, they might hide them. In addition, a leak to the public might start a huge panic. Therefore, the president made every effort to appear that everything was running normally in the White House.

On October 16, at 9:30 A.M., President Kennedy enjoyed a visit with astronaut Walter Schirra, who had just completed a mission in which he orbited Earth six times. Kennedy met next with the White House Panel

President Kennedy (right) met with astronaut Walter Schirra and his family during the Cuban Missile Crisis. Kennedy kept his previously scheduled appointments, believing it was important to keep up an appearance of business as usual.

on Mental Retardation. In both situations, Kennedy was an enthusiastic participant, showing no sign of the crisis that was going on.

When President Kennedy was finally able to meet with the ExCom, his advisors had determined that there was a medium-range ballistic missile launch site and two military encampments already built on Cuba.

Missile expert Sidney Graybeal said there were two types of missiles in the photographs. The first was about sixty-seven feet long and had a range of 630 to 700 miles. The second was about seventy-three feet long and had a range of approximately eleven hundred miles. Because Cuba was only ninety miles away, these weapons would be a clear threat to the United States if they were armed with nuclear warheads.[2]

The First Photographs

To many on the ExCom, the photographs were less dramatic than the crisis itself. Robert Kennedy later recollected:

> Photographs were shown to us. Experts arrived with their charts and pointers and told us that if we looked carefully, we could see there was a missile base being constructed in a field near San Cristolbal, Cuba. I, for one, had to take their word for it. . . . What I saw appeared to be no more than the clearing of a field for a farm or the basement of a home. I was relieved to hear later that this was the same reaction of virtually everyone at the meeting, including President Kennedy.[3]

Despite their untrained eyes, the ExCom tried to understand the information they were shown. Secretary of Defense Robert McNamara wanted to know if there were any evidence confirming that there were nuclear warheads on the island. "The time between today and the time when the readiness-to-fire capability develops is a very important thing," said McNamara.[4] None of the photos showed warheads. If there were no warheads, then the missiles in the photographs were no more dangerous than an unloaded gun. However, there was a possibility that warheads were on the island, but had not yet been detected by the surveillance flights. If so, they could soon be mounted onto the missiles. The United States could not afford to remain idle.

Considering the Options

Four possible ways to resolve the problem were considered by the ExCom. The first was a general air strike, or bombing, of all the missile sites. The second was an air strike that would target the missiles and other weapons, such as MiG-21 fighter jets and SAM sites, in Cuba. The third option was an invasion of Cuba, which ExCom believed would take eight days to prepare. The fourth was a naval blockade of Cuba to try to prevent the arrival of nuclear warheads and more missiles.

Kennedy's initial preference was for the first air strike.[5] A simple attack to destroy the missiles seemed like the best action to take. However, there would be five days of discussions before the president would make a final decision.

The end of the first briefing of the ExCom left everyone feeling very uneasy. The missiles in Cuba put the United States in a direct confrontation with the Soviet Union. A confrontation could become a war. War could involve nuclear weapons.

However, even at this early stage of the crisis, President Kennedy displayed the best of his leadership abilities. "The president never panicked, never shuddered, his hands never shook," recalled Arthur Lundahl. "He was crisp and businesslike and speedy in his remarks and he issued them with clarity and dispatch, as though he were dispatching a train or a set of instructions to an office group." General Maxwell Taylor also praised Kennedy's demeanor: "Kennedy gave no evidence of shock or trepidation [hesitation] resulting from the threat to the nation . . . but rather a deep controlled anger at the duplicity of the Soviet officials who had tried to deceive him."[6]

During the briefing, President Kennedy issued his first order during the crisis: an increase in the number of U-2 flights over Cuba. "I want the photography interpreted and the findings from the readouts as soon as possible," said the president.[7] The ExCom would meet again later that afternoon. In the meantime, the ExCom would keep its discussions top-secret. Everyone would pretend that nothing unusual was happening. The president went to his next appointment, a formal luncheon with the Crown Prince of Libya.

Narrowing Down the Choices

The second meeting of the ExCom began at 6:30 P.M. It was a discussion of possible actions to take. The president still preferred an air strike against the missiles.

When new reports revealed more missile sites in Cuba, the Joint Chiefs of Staff—President Kennedy's military advisors—were concerned. They were afraid that a small strike would not be enough to end the crisis. They suggested a more extensive air attack.

Others, such as Secretary of State Dean Rusk, felt that any air strike would only lead to a more complicated situation. He had already pointed out an article in the previous day's *The New York Times*. It quoted some Soviet officials as saying, "We'll trade Cuba for Berlin."[8]

Secretary of Defense Robert McNamara supported a naval blockade around Cuba. He believed a blockade would demonstrate American decisiveness and military strength, and would still allow for a possible peaceful resolution to the crisis.

Although no firm decision was made, the general feeling of the ExCom was in favor of some kind of air strike against Cuba. An attack was tentatively scheduled for October 20, the following Saturday.[9]

As the ExCom continued to consider its options, Kennedy's policy of maintaining "business as usual" appearances kept the Soviets guessing. By Wednesday, October 17, the Soviets thought it was likely that the United States had found out about the missiles in

Cuba. However, there had been no American reaction. Perhaps, the Soviets thought, the United States had no objection to the installation of the missiles.[10]

The Soviets Wonder What the Americans Know

Without a clear understanding of what the Americans knew, Khrushchev maintained his own appearances. He met with the new American ambassador in Moscow, Foy Kohler, on the morning of October 16. In their discussion, Khrushchev continued to refer to the Soviet military buildup in Cuba as a defensive operation. On the same day, a Soviet diplomat delivered a secret message from Khrushchev to Robert Kennedy, to be passed on to the president. It reassured the president that no Soviet surface-to-surface missiles would be installed in Cuba.[11]

The next day, an opportunity came up for the Soviets to get a better understanding of what the Americans were thinking. Before the Cuban Missile Crisis began, Soviet Foreign Minister Andrei Gromyko had scheduled a meeting with President Kennedy for 5:00 P.M. on Thursday, October 18. While Gromyko was not going to raise the subject of the missiles, he was curious to see if the president would indicate whether he knew of the Soviets' activities in Cuba.

Prior to his appointment, Gromyko met with Soviet Ambassador Anatoly Dobrynin to discuss the latest information they had on the Kennedy administration. Dobrynin, who had not been informed about the Soviet missiles in Cuba, told Gromyko that he believed the United States no longer had any plans to invade Cuba. The Kennedy administration expected, Dobrynin explained, that if the United States attacked Cuba, the Soviet Union would respond by attacking an American ally somewhere else in the world.[12] Gromyko left for his meeting with Kennedy feeling confident about meeting with his opponents.

The Cubans were also at ease. On the previous night, Fidel Castro had dinner with his ally Ahmed Ben Bella of Algeria, who had recently been on a diplomatic visit to the United States. Ben Bella told Castro that he had a conversation with the president. Kennedy had said, "the U.S. government does not have any plans to intervene militarily in Cuba."[13] Hearing this and having the security of Soviet missiles within his borders gave Castro reason to relax.

More Photographs for the ExCom

Events prior to Kennedy's meeting with Gromyko were a very different experience for the ExCom. At the ExCom's 11:00 A.M. meeting, the latest photos had uncovered the most disturbing news of the week. They indicated that there were Soviet missiles in Cuba that had enough range to target American ICBM bases in the midwestern United States, farther than was originally thought. The ExCom concluded that, with one missile strike, the Soviets wanted to be able to attack major American cities with millions of people as well as destroy the United States' ability to retaliate.[14]

This new information changed the minds of many ExCom members. General Maxwell Taylor, chairman of the Joint Chiefs of Staff said to the president, "We consider nothing short of a full invasion [of Cuba], as practical military action."[15] Ambassador Llewellyn Thompson suggested that the invasion be preceded by a naval blockade in order to stir a public demand for the removal of the Soviet missiles. President Kennedy, however, believed that the blockade would only help Castro by giving him time to prepare the weapons he had. Despite the possibility that military action could escalate into nuclear war, most of the ExCom, including the president, at that moment, supported an invasion of Cuba.[16] Before he could come to a final decision, however, the president left with Secretary of State Dean Rusk and Ambassador Llewellyn Thompson for their meeting with Gromyko and Dobrynin.

President Kennedy Meets With the Soviets

The exchange between the statesmen was tense. Neither side revealed more than necessary. Both sides wanted to know more.

They talked about Berlin first. Then Gromyko brought up the subject of Cuba. He restated that the Soviets were only aiding Cuba's defense.

President Kennedy remained expressionless as he listened. When Gromyko said that the Soviets were concerned that the United States was planning another invasion, Kennedy grew angry. He denied that he had any such intention.

In an attempt to draw some kind of information out of Gromyko, the president said that it was the Soviets who had set out on a course that was of considerable concern to the United States. This was a very subtle reference to the missiles in Cuba. He asked Gromyko if he understood his concern. Gromyko answered, "Perfectly."[17]

Before the meeting ended, the president repeated his warnings of September 4 and September 13. He told the Soviet Union that "the gravest of issues would arise" if any offensive weapons were found in Cuba.[18]

President Kennedy met with Soviet Foreign Minister Andrei Gromyko (next to Kennedy), Ambassador Anatoly Dobrynin, and a Soviet assistant during the Cuban Missile Crisis.

The meeting between Gromyko and Kennedy was a continuation of the charade both sides were playing during the Cuban Missile Crisis. Kennedy was angry that high-ranking Soviet officials were lying to him. However, Gromyko did not feel he was lying because Kennedy did not ask him directly about the missiles in Cuba.[19]

Later that evening, the Soviet foreign minister filed a report to Moscow. In it, he wrote, "the situation [with the United States] is . . . wholly satisfactory."[20] Little did he know that President Kennedy was now contemplating an all-out invasion of Cuba.

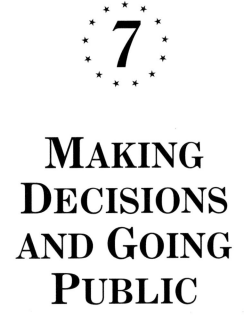

By Friday, October 19, it appeared that the president's week would come to an unproductive end. Little progress had been made since the discovery of the missiles in Cuba over the previous weekend. His meeting with Andrei Gromyko and Anatoly Dobrynin had left the impression that talking directly with the Soviets would not solve the problem. Just

MAKING DECISIONS AND GOING PUBLIC

as troubling was the fact that, after days of meetings, the ExCom had not yet made a clear decision about what to do. A decision had to be made soon.

The President Leaves the ExCom

In order to help the ExCom reach its goal, President Kennedy made plans to be away for a few days. He believed that, by continuing his campaign schedule, he would not only maintain the appearance that everything was normal, but also allow the ExCom to exchange ideas more freely, without the somewhat intimidating presence of the president. On the morning of October 19, President Kennedy left for Chicago. He put his brother Robert in charge of the ExCom.[1]

Young boys were thrilled to meet the president on a campaign stop in Chicago just days after the missiles were discovered in Cuba.

The ExCom spent the day narrowing its options down to two choices. Then, its members divided into two groups. One group favored using an air strike. It included McGeorge Bundy, John McCone, Dean Acheson, and Attorney General Robert Kennedy. The second group supported a naval blockade. It included Robert McNamara, Dean Rusk, and Llewellyn Thompson. Each group had an assignment: Write a paper by the end of the day explaining why its plan was the better one.

The result of the two groups' work was a thorough examination of the strengths and weaknesses of each option. An air strike would be quick and decisive, and would make the United States appear to be a strong nation that would not tolerate any threats to its security. However, an air strike would be expensive and there was no guarantee that it would be completely successful. Also, to use force without warning might hurt relations with the United States' allies. Some members of the ExCom were concerned that the United States would look aggressive. Using a blockade would allow for the problem to be solved through diplomacy. There would be little chance of loss of life. However, many ExCom members questioned whether it would be effective. By the day's end, the papers were ready for the president's review.

President Kennedy Makes His First Move

Decision making became easier after the events of the next morning. A report from Ray Cline of the CIA confirmed that there were eight MRBMs that could be fired from Cuba to the United States that very day. Although there was still no evidence that nuclear warheads were on the island, Cline feared that they were either somewhere in an undiscovered spot in Cuba, or they were going to be delivered to Cuba soon.[2] Cline's report prompted Robert Kennedy to call the president in Chicago to tell him to return to the ExCom.

The fear that military action against Cuba could trigger the Soviet Union to launch a nuclear attack prevailed over the ExCom. Robert Kennedy switched sides in the debate. He joined those who favored the naval blockade, rather than an air strike. Adlai Stevenson, the United States ambassador to the United Nations, joined this session of the ExCom. He, too, favored the blockade.

Finally, when the president had returned, the ExCom voted on a course of action. The decision was made. The United States would use a naval blockade to stop any ship bringing offensive weapons to Cuba.

The president would address the nation on television and radio, informing the public about the crisis and what the administration was doing about it. At that time, the Soviets would learn that their Operation Anadyr had been discovered.[3]

The President Faces His Critics

Not everyone was happy about the president's decision. During the meeting, President Kennedy turned to General Maxwell Taylor and said, "I know that you and your colleagues are unhappy with the decision, but I trust that you will support me in this decision." Taylor assured him that, although they did not agree, the military would support the president.[4]

Kennedy faced harsher criticism when he met with leaders from the United States Congress on the morning of Monday, October 22. Senator Richard Russell, chairman of the Senate Armed Services Committee, believed the whole crisis was Khrushchev's scheme to test the nation's will. Russell clearly disagreed with the president, and began to pressure him:

I don't see how we are going to get any stronger or get in any better position to meet this threat. . . . We're either a first-class power or we're not. . . . You have warned [the Soviets] time and again. . . . The Secretary of State says: "Give them time to pause and think." They'll use that time to pause and think, to get better prepared. . . . I think that the more that we [avoid using the military], the more surely [Khrushchev] is to convince himself that we are afraid to make any real movement and to really fight.[5]

The president remained firm in his decision. He was not against using the military at some point. In fact, he had raised the level of military alert to the third level of defense condition, or "DEFCON 3." Bombers at airfields all over the United States and at bases around the world were loaded with nuclear weapons. The United States' ICBMs, about 132 missiles, were prepared to fire. Other American missiles in allied nations in Europe were also prepared. Nuclear submarines took their positions in the North Atlantic Ocean.[6]

However, President Kennedy was against a military air strike as a first step. He could not be certain that an air strike would destroy all the missiles in Cuba. Reconnaissance missions kept returning with new information about more sites. Kennedy was not willing to take the chance of using force, only to find out later that some sites had remained hidden. Also, with the blockade, loss of life could be avoided for the time being, and diplomatic discussions with the Soviets would be possible. Ambassador Llewellyn Thompson bluntly advised that the Soviets would regard an air strike against its missile bases, which would kill between four and five thousand people in the crossfire, as worse than stopping their ships.[7]

While no one knew how Khrushchev would respond to the blockade, it was expected that he would, in turn, blockade Berlin as Stalin had done in 1948. As Kennedy met with congressional leaders, he referred to a letter from British Prime Minister Harold Macmillan that said, "If he [Khrushchev] reacts outside the Caribbean . . . it will be tempting for him to answer one blockade by declaring another."[8]

This may have been one of the reasons the president wanted to use the word *quarantine*, rather than *blockade*. A blockade was an act of war.[9] Kennedy hoped using a different word would make the action seem less aggressive. No matter what term was used, however, preventing Soviet ships from reaching Cuba would be considered a violation of international law by Khrushchev. That is, it would go against the behavior generally accepted and followed by the nations of the world.

Though President Kennedy expected Khrushchev to blockade Berlin, he could not be certain of it. The quarantine was the United States' first step in a complicated crisis. "So we start here," said the president. "We don't know where [Khrushchev's] going to take us or where we're going to take ourselves."[10]

Fear of War Builds

As Kennedy prepared his address to the nation, Khrushchev was feeling uneasy. His sources had informed him that the president was going to make a speech, but they did not know what issues he would raise. Khrushchev and his advisors, a body of the Soviet government called the Presidium, had a feeling that Kennedy would talk about Cuba. The Soviet premier did not trust the latest report from his foreign minister, Andrei Gromyko. The report said that United States military action against Cuba was "almost beyond belief," based on his meeting with the president last Thursday evening.[11] Khrushchev feared that Gromyko had been fooled, and that Kennedy was preparing an invasion.

"The thing is we were not going to unleash war," said Khrushchev, speaking about the intention of Operation Anadyr. "We just wanted to intimidate them, to deter the anti-Cuban forces." He was just as frightened about the prospect of a conflict that could escalate into a nuclear war as anyone in the White House.[12]

The Nation Learns About the Crisis

President Kennedy went on television at 7:00 P.M. Eastern Daylight Time on Monday, October 22, to deliver a message that was clear and serious. "This Government, as promised, has maintained the closest surveillance of the Soviet military buildup on the island of Cuba," he began. "Within the past week,

President Kennedy addressed the nation in a speech broadcast from the Oval Office.

unmistakable evidence has established the fact that a series of offensive missile sites is now in preparation on that imprisoned island."[13]

Kennedy outlined the danger. "Each of these missiles," he said, "is capable of striking Washington, D.C., the Panama Canal, Cape Canaveral, Mexico City, or any other city in the southeastern part of the United States, in Central America, or in the Caribbean area." He explained that the intermediate-range ballistic missile sites were capable of reaching most major cities "as

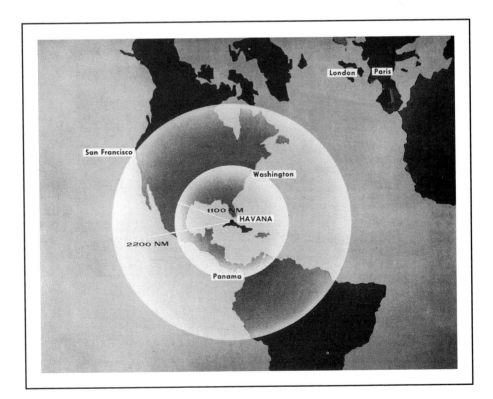

The Soviet medium-range ballistic missiles in Cuba could easily reach much of the United States.

far north as Hudson Bay, Canada and as far south as Lima, Peru."[14]

This was a speech that few Americans had believed they would ever hear. Americans had seen the bombings of Japan. They had seen the Soviet Union challenge them in the arms race. Nuclear tests had been conducted often since World War II. American children had even grown up with "duck and cover" drills. Still, an actual nuclear war seemed to be a remote possibility until Kennedy gave his speech. Even the way he was speaking, without his characteristic smile, showed that this was a very serious situation.

President Kennedy described his plan:

> All ships of any kind bound for Cuba from whatever nation or port will, if found to contain cargoes of offensive weapons, be turned back. . . . We are not at this time, however, denying the necessities of life as the Soviets attempted to do in their Berlin blockade of 1948.[15]

Surveillance would be increased, the United States military put on alert, and diplomatic organizations would be used to help bring about the "prompt dismantling and withdrawal of all offensive weapons in Cuba."[16]

The president closed with an appeal to Khrushchev:

> I call upon Chairman Khrushchev to halt and eliminate this clandestine [deceptively secret], reckless, and provocative threat to world peace and to stable relations between our two nations. I call upon him further to abandon this course of world domination, and to join in an historic effort to end the perilous arms race and transform the history of man.[17]

A copy of President Kennedy's speech was later delivered to the Kremlin, the government center in the Soviet Union. It came with a candid letter from Kennedy to Khrushchev:

> [T]he one thing that has most concerned me has been the possibility that your Government would not correctly understand the will and determination of the United States in any given situation, since I have not assumed that you or any other sane man would, in this nuclear age, deliberately plunge the world into war in which it is crystal clear no country could win and which could only result in catastrophic consequences to the whole world, including the aggressor. . . . I wish to point out that the action we are taking is the minimum necessary to remove the threat to the security of the nations of this hemisphere. . . . I hope that your Government will refrain from any action which would widen or deepen this already grave crisis. . . .[18]

News of Kennedy's speech left Khrushchev relieved. Because the president did not intend to invade Cuba, Khrushchev did not intend to change his plans. As President Kennedy was making his address, thirty Soviet ships were on their way to Cuba. One of them, the *Aleksandrovsk*, was carrying nuclear warheads. The Soviet leader would neither respect the quarantine, nor would he call his ships back home.[19]

BRINKMANSHIP

The president's speech did not start a widespread panic around the country, but it did leave many Americans feeling very tense. There were signs of the hard times that the president had said lay ahead. People bought extra food, gasoline, and anything else they thought they might need in the event of war. Televisions carried images of military personnel practicing maneuvers. Meanwhile, the Reverend Billy Graham preached to a crowd of ten thousand people a sermon called "The End of the World."[1] Beneath the people's reactions to the crisis was the fact that no one knew how Khrushchev would respond to the quarantine.

Khrushchev Reacts

As Kennedy sent six more U-2 flights over Cuba, Khrushchev contemplated his response to the president's address and private message. He decided to use a type of diplomacy called brinkmanship, which was practiced by both the Soviet Union and the United States during the Cold War. It was presumed that neither side wanted a nuclear war, because a nuclear war was not winnable. However, by bringing a situation to the brink of nuclear war, the opponent might be compelled to give in to the other nation's interests.

SOURCE DOCUMENT

DURING THE MISSILE CRISIS OF '62 I WAS IN SEVENTH GRADE. . . . I REMEMBER THAT THERE WAS A LOT OF TENSION, THERE WAS AN HORRENDOUS AMOUNT OF TENSION. I KNOW THAT MY MOTHER WAS VERY FRIGHTENED AND TENSE AND EVERYBODY REALLY WAS, AND YOU KNOW, PEOPLE WERE GLUED TO THE TELEVISION, BUT NATURALLY I WENT TO SCHOOL THE FOLLOWING DAY AS EVERYBODY TRIED TO GO ALONG WITH THEIR LIVES AND I REMEMBER I WAS IN THE BATHROOM OF THE SCHOOL . . . WHEN THEY SAID OVER THE LOUDSPEAKER THAT EVERYONE . . . HAD TO RETURN TO THEIR HOMEROOMS IMMEDIATELY AND GET INSTRUCTION FROM THEIR HOMEROOM TEACHER. AND IT WAS PROBABLY ONE OF THE SCARIEST MOMENTS OF MY LIFE. . . .[2]

Many Americans today can still remember the fear they felt during the Cuban Missile Crisis.

Khrushchev's response was to try to scare President Kennedy by saying his actions could provoke a nuclear war:

> You, Mr. President, are not declaring quarantines, but advancing an ultimatum and threatening that unless we subordinate ourselves to your demands, you will use force. . . . the Soviet Government considers that violation of freedom of the use of international waters and international air space as an act of aggression, pushing mankind towards the abyss of a world missile-nuclear war.[3]

Khrushchev also protested the quarantine. "United States has openly taken path . . . of aggressive actions both against Cuba and against Soviet Union," wrote

Khrushchev to Kennedy.[4] To Khrushchev, the quarantine was a violation of international law. He warned that Soviet ships may not respect it. Khrushchev also maintained that any Soviet arms were there solely to defend Cuba, and that the United States had misunderstood the reasons for the missiles.[5]

The Quarantine Begins

President Kennedy had anticipated Khrushchev's protesting the quarantine on the basis of international law. In the days prior to Kennedy's television address, the president decided to seek the approval of the OAS and the United Nations for the quarantine. Although the president had told congressional leaders that he was prepared to go forward with the quarantine even without the support of these peacekeeping organizations, he expected to get their backing.

President Kennedy's instincts were correct. On Tuesday, October 23, the OAS voted unanimously in favor of the quarantine. At the United Nations, American Ambassador Adlai Stevenson tried to win the support of the rest of the world. In a speech he delivered at the United Nations Security Council, Stevenson said:

> When the Soviet Union['s] . . . actions are in flagrant violation of the policies of the Organization of American States and of the Charter of the United Nations, this clearly is a threat to this hemisphere. And when it thus upsets the precarious balance in the world, it is a threat to the whole world.[6]

Soviet Ambassador Valerian Zorin denied Stevenson's charges. He argued that there were only defensive weapons in Cuba. He did not, however, address the presence of the ballistic missiles. The Soviet Union had not yet made any public acknowledgment of them.[7]

With the support of the United States' allies, President John F. Kennedy signed the Proclamation of Interdiction on October 23. The United States Navy would begin forming a blockade around Cuba at 10:00 A.M. the next day. As the president signed the proclamation, however, the Soviet vessel *Aleksandrovsk* had docked safely in Cuba with its cargo of nuclear warheads. The threat of a nuclear attack against the United States had never before been so real.[8]

The Robert Kennedy–Anatoly Dobrynin Connection

Second to the prospect of a nuclear war, the thought that troubled the Kennedy administration most was that they had been deceived by the Soviets. One man who felt particularly betrayed was Robert Kennedy, who had a special diplomatic relationship with Soviet Ambassador Anatoly Dobrynin. Throughout John F. Kennedy's presidency, these two men had conducted private conversations. Robert Kennedy believed these talks had led to a greater understanding between their two nations. However, during the Cuban Missile Crisis, Robert Kennedy felt like a fool who had trusted his Soviet contact too easily. After the president had given his Monday night speech, he suggested that the

The president signs the order to form a naval quarantine around Cuba.

attorney general confront Ambassador Dobrynin. Robert Kennedy went to the Soviet Embassy late in the evening on Tuesday, October 23.

"You . . . particularly told me about the defensive goals behind the supply of Soviet arms . . . at the time of our meeting at the beginning of September," said Robert Kennedy. "I told this to the president, who was satisfied with this policy of the Soviet government."[9] Ambassador Dobrynin asked why, if the president had concerns about weapons in Cuba, he did not raise the issue when he met with Andrei Gromyko on the previous Thursday. Gromyko had merely repeated the same lie, answered Robert Kennedy, even though the president knew about the missiles.

Dobrynin was able to calm the attorney general by telling him that his bosses in Moscow only told him what they wanted him to know. He had not known about the missiles and had been misled by Khrushchev and Gromyko. Kennedy believed him. Before leaving, Kennedy asked what he thought the Soviet ships would do once they ran into the quarantine. "They must not submit to any illegal demands on the high seas," said Dobrynin.

"I don't know how all this will end," replied Kennedy, "but we intend to stop your ships."[10]

Khrushchev Rallies His Supporters

As the quarantine was forming on Wednesday, October 24, Nikita Khrushchev felt very confident about his position in the crisis. The *Aleksandrovsk* had completed its mission just hours before the quarantine began. The missile sites in Cuba, complete with nuclear warheads, were nearly operational.

On the same day, Khrushchev would make an effort to seem like a peacemaker who was trying to end the crisis. He readily accepted a proposal from Secretary General of the United Nations U Thant. The proposal called upon the Soviet Union to stop its shipments of weapons to Cuba, and for the United States to drop its quarantine. However, President Kennedy was just as ready to reject the United Nations' proposal, insisting that the Soviet Union dismantle its missiles in Cuba.[11]

Khrushchev also began showing interest in holding a meeting with President Kennedy to negotiate a peaceful end to the crisis. He first mentioned a meeting in an open letter to famous pacifist philosopher Lord Bertrand Russell. However, in an unexpected move, Khrushchev also called upon American businessman William Knox, who happened to be doing business in Moscow that week. He asked Knox to deliver a private message to President Kennedy. In it, he admitted, for the first time, that he had placed the ballistic missiles in Cuba. He suggested that the two leaders meet.[12]

Khrushchev Tests the Quarantine

Even though these actions seemed to be friendly, Khrushchev's actions on the sea made the United States nervous. On the same morning, most of the

Soviet vessels bound for Cuba had been given orders from the Kremlin to stop, slow down, or reverse course before reaching the quarantine. Two ships maintained a distance of ninety miles away from the line of interdiction, the boundary in the Atlantic Ocean that defined the quarantine. Only one, the oil tanker *Bucharest*, stayed on course toward Cuba. It carried no weapons.

Beneath the ocean surface, a Soviet submarine had positioned itself between the quarantine and the Soviet vessels. An aircraft carrier, the U.S.S. *Essex*, was

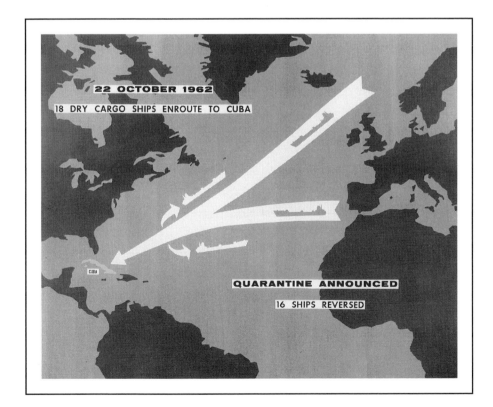

A CIA illustration of the naval quarantine.

dispatched to counter the submarine. The approach of the *Bucharest* signaled that the first test of the quarantine was only hours away. The United States military alert was raised from DEFCON 3 to DEFCON 2. A condition of DEFCON 1, the highest state of preparedness, usually meant that the United States was at war.[13]

Khrushchev's Decision

On the evening of October 24, the White House played its own game of brinkmanship. Having received Khrushchev's message, which accused Kennedy of pushing the world toward nuclear war, at about 9:00 P.M., Kennedy knew that a quick response was needed. After working late with his staff, the president sent his reply at 2:00 A.M. the next day.

The message disappointed Khrushchev. He had expected Kennedy to back down. Instead, the president reminded Khrushchev that the United States government had been quite clear. It would not tolerate offensive weapons in Cuba. He also reviewed all the Soviet government's statements that had assured the United States that the weapons were strictly defensive. "And then I learned beyond doubt," wrote the president, "that all these public assurances were false." Kennedy ended his message by placing the burden of ending the crisis on Khrushchev: "I ask you to recognize clearly, Mr. Chairman, that it was not I who issued the first challenge in this case. . . . I hope that your government will take the necessary action to permit a restoration of the earlier situation."[14] The message did not make any mention of Khrushchev's willingness to work with the United Nations, nor his efforts for a meeting. It seemed that Khrushchev's brinkmanship had backfired.

Other news also disturbed Khrushchev. The KGB, the Soviet equivalent of the CIA, said that the United States had raised its level of military alert. There were reports that American hospitals were preparing to receive casualties. Another informant brought news that the United States Strategic Air Command, a special division of the air force specializing in nuclear war, was on alert. All these factors reinforced the severity of Kennedy's message. It became clear to Khrushchev that he could not keep the missiles in Cuba without going to war.

Behind closed doors, Khrushchev made some major decisions. "We must dismantle the missiles to make Cuba into a zone of peace," Khrushchev told his advisors.[15] Previously, he had hoped to get four more missile transports to Cuba. The change in the situation compelled him to give the order for them to turn around.

Khrushchev saw a possible end to the crisis. In exchange for dismantling the missiles, he would demand that the United States would give a pledge not to invade Cuba. This was not exactly in keeping with the goals of Operation Anadyr, but the Presidium approved the plan and hoped that Khrushchev could succeed.

"Comrades, let's go to the Bolshoi Theater this evening," said the chairman to his advisors. Khrushchev had a very good reason to treat his colleagues to a night out at one of the world's most famous opera houses. "Our own people as well as foreign eyes will notice, and perhaps it will calm them down," he said. The idea was that, if Khrushchev and other leaders could be seen relaxing and enjoying themselves, then there must not be much cause for alarm. However, years later in his memoirs, Khrushchev admitted, "We were trying to disguise our own anxiety, which was intense."[16]

A Way out of the Cuban Missile Crisis

On the same day that Khrushchev decided to dismantle his missiles in Cuba, an article appeared in *The New York Times*. It, too, offered a possible end to the Cuban Missile Crisis. Written by journalist Walter Lippmann, the article examined President Kennedy's options. Lippmann suggested that Kennedy dismantle United States Jupiter missiles in Turkey that were aimed at the Soviet Union. The missiles were, in fact, obsolete, since the United States had developed more sophisticated weapons. However, because Turkey was about as far from the Soviet Union as Cuba was from the United States, removing the missiles could be a trade that would help end the crisis. One of the many readers of Lippmann's column was Nikita Khrushchev.

Lippmann was not the first to make this suggestion. On the previous Sunday, the day after the decision was made to use the naval quarantine, President Kennedy spoke with British ambassador and longtime Kennedy family friend David Ormsby-Gore about the possible closing of the missile base in Turkey. Robert Kennedy, in a private meeting in the Justice Department, concluded that "the Turkish missiles would have to be given up" in order to end the crisis. The attorney general, however, had concerns about dismantling the missiles publicly. He feared that the nation would appear weak.[17]

The approach of the Soviet tanker *Bucharest* toward the line of interdiction was an example of just how cautious both sides in the crisis had become. This was the first Soviet ship to reach the line, but it did not carry any weapons. Khrushchev knew that a ship carrying weapons would force the United States to react. Yet he still maintained his nation's right to use the free seas and deliver a basic necessity (oil) to Cuba. At the same time, the United States was faced with maintaining the quarantine without provoking the Soviet Union to take action.

An American ship in the blockade radioed the *Bucharest*, telling it to identify itself and its cargo. The *Bucharest* promptly replied. Even though the military wanted to board and inspect the ship as a show of strength, President Kennedy gave the order to allow the *Bucharest* to proceed to Cuba. There was no need for a confrontation yet. Kennedy wanted to give the Soviets time to consider the circumstances.

Showdown at the United Nations

In the diplomatic arena, however, the United States would not be so lenient. Although Nikita Khrushchev had privately admitted to the president that he had placed missiles in Cuba for defensive purposes, the Soviets had not yet done so publicly. As late as Thursday, October 25, after aerial photographs of the missile sites appeared in many of the world's newspapers, high-ranking Soviet officials were saying that all Soviet weapons in Cuba were strictly defensive. This stance would prove to be a blunder for Soviet

Another U-2 photo taken later in the crisis showed more details of the Soviet arms in Cuba.

Ambassador Valerian Zorin. At the meeting of the United Nations Security Council, he was confronted by the United States Ambassador Adlai Stevenson, who had entered the meeting prepared to win the support of the member nations of the United Nations.

"All right, sir, let me ask you one simple question," said Stevenson. "Do you . . . deny that the USSR has placed and is placing medium- and intermediate-range missiles and sites in Cuba?" Stevenson, aware of the audience and television cameras in the room, was aggressive. "Yes or no—don't wait for the translation—yes or no."[18]

Zorin tried to fend off Stevenson's attack. "I am not standing in the dock of an American court," replied Zorin, "and I shall not answer at this stage."[19]

Stevenson would not relent. "You are in the courtroom of world opinion right now and you can answer yes or no," he said.[20] Even when Zorin tried to take control of the proceedings by telling Stevenson to finish his speech, Stevenson persisted. Zorin told him that he would have his answer "in due course."

Stevenson took off his glasses, backed away from the table, and said, "I am prepared to wait for my answer until hell freezes over, if that is your decision."[21] The room filled with laughter.

Zorin smiled sheepishly and again tried to regain control of the meeting. This time, he gave the floor to the representative from Chile. The room swelled with more laughter when the Chilean ambassador refused to speak because he wanted to hear Zorin's answer to Stevenson's question.

Stevenson then answered his own question for the Security Council. An assistant brought enlarged photographs of the missile sites in Cuba. After Stevenson had explained the content of the photographs, he convinced the Security Council of the danger in Cuba. "We know the facts, and so do you, sir [addressing Zorin], and we are ready to talk about them," said Stevenson. "Our job here is not to score debating points. Our job . . . is to save the peace. And if you are ready to try, we are."[22]

While this exchange between Stevenson and Zorin was dramatic, it did little to resolve the crisis. Zorin had no authority to negotiate with anyone, and no new suggestions were made as a result of this confrontation. Stevenson's performance was applauded by many, including the president, but others would later criticize him for being undiplomatic. In the end, the United Nations Security Council would not play any role in bringing an end to the Cuban Missile Crisis.

While Valerian Zorin verbally jousted with Adlai Stevenson in the Security Council, both John F. Kennedy and Nikita Khrushchev had received a second message from U Thant, secretary general of the United Nations. He requested that both leaders avoid a direct confrontation at the quarantine's line of interdiction. Both Kennedy and Khrushchev agreed. Neither leader wanted to provoke the other.

9

THE MOST DANGEROUS DAYS OF THE COLD WAR

One vessel, the *Marucla*, a Lebanese vessel carrying dry goods to Cuba, was sailing under a Soviet charter. It was stopped and inspected by the United States Navy. The crew was cooperative, the cargo harmless, and the ship was allowed to proceed to Cuba. Interestingly, one of the two American destroyers that stopped the *Marucla* was named the U.S.S. *Joseph P. Kennedy, Jr.*, after the president's brother who had been killed during World War II. The *Marucla* was the only ship ever to be boarded and inspected by the United States during the crisis.

Preparing for War

While both sides in the crisis were very careful not to start a military conflict, they still prepared for the real possibility of war. A large concentration of military forces assembled in the southeastern United States. Kennedy's Joint Chiefs of Staff developed a plan that would hit Cuba with a massive air strike only twelve hours after the president's order. The bombings would continue for seven days, after which United States soldiers would invade the island.[1]

Meanwhile, CIA reports indicated that the Soviets were not remaining idle. The pace of the construction of the Cuban missile sites had quickened. Efforts to camouflage the sites were also improved. If not for photos taken on missions early in October, the United States might have missed them.[2] At 6:15 P.M. on Friday, October 26, Kennedy's Press Secretary Pierre Salinger relayed this information to the press: "There is evidence that . . . considerable construction activity was being engaged in at the intermediate range ballistic missile sites. Bulldozers and cranes were observed . . . clearing new areas within the sites and improving the approach roads to the launch pads."[3]

Rumors at the National Press Club

Khrushchev's worries about American military activities were heightened by a rumor that one of his spies reported. Khrushchev had a couple of KGB agents who were posing as Soviet journalists in Washington, D.C. One such agent was Anatoly Gorsky, a correspondent for the Soviet national news service, as well as a KGB officer who reported to the Soviet Embassy in Washington. As a member of the National Press Club in Washington, D.C., Gorsky was a regular customer at the club's bar.

At about 10:00 P.M. on Wednesday evening, a club bartender, who was a native Russian, overheard a conversation between two journalists for the *New York Herald*. One of them, Warren Rodgers, was going to be sent to Cuba to cover the American invasion. Believing that the United States government had already made a decision to use force against Cuba, the bartender contacted Gorsky. Gorsky informed his superior, Aleksandr Feklisov, at the Soviet Embassy. After reporting the conversation to Moscow, Feklisov participated in one of the strangest episodes of the Cuban Missile Crisis.

The Noninvasion Pledge

Feklisov, who lived under the alias of Alexander Fomin, contacted an American acquaintance to join him for lunch on Friday, October 26. The American was John Scali, host of the ABC news program *Issues and Answers*. He and Feklisov met occasionally to talk and help improve Feklisov's English. It had been some time since Scali had heard from Feklisov, but under the circumstances of the crisis, he was very willing to meet with his Soviet colleague.

Scali could not have predicted what took place over lunch. Feklisov appeared to be deeply troubled by the threat of an American invasion of Cuba. He gave Scali a set of terms to end the crisis. The three-point plan said the Soviets would dismantle their missile bases, Castro would not accept any offensive weapons in Cuba, and the United States would promise never to invade Cuba. Feklisov suggested that Scali bring the terms to the State Department to see what they thought of the offer.[4] He further suggested that, if Adlai Stevenson introduced the offer at the United Nations, the Soviet delegates would agree to it.[5] Feklisov even gave Scali his home telephone number to make sure he could be contacted if necessary.

The State Department welcomed Scali's message. It seemed to be the first real attempt to bring an end to the crisis. Dean Rusk also knew that Feklisov was a KGB officer. Rusk suspected that perhaps Khrushchev was really behind the offer. While Scali did not have the authority to make any official agreements, Dean Rusk sent him back to meet with Feklisov and tell him that there was reason to believe the United States government saw real possibilities in his suggested end to the crisis.[6]

A Peculiar Message Reaches the President

Later that evening, the White House received another curious message from the Soviets. It was a long, personal letter from Nikita Khrushchev to President Kennedy. It took more than six hours for the entire message to be cabled from Moscow to Washington. The unexpected message was not like the typical messages that world leaders exchanged. It revealed a sincere, thoughtful, and possibly frightened Nikita Khrushchev whom no one in the ExCom had ever known before.

Khrushchev wanted to avoid war. He appealed to President Kennedy to understand his exact feelings. "War is our enemy and a calamity for all of the peoples. . . . I have participated in two wars and I know that war ends when it has rolled through cities and villages, everywhere sowing death and destruction," wrote the chairman.[7]

That did not mean that Khrushchev had changed his point of view. "You are mistaken if you think that any of our means on Cuba are offensive," he said.[8] He compared the missiles with a simple cannon. If a cannon is positioned on a nation's boundary, he said, it is defensive. However, if it is placed in front of a regiment and used to clear the way for the troops that follow it, it is offensive.

The part of the message that most interested the ExCom reflected the offer delivered by John Scali. Khrushchev reviewed his nation's alliance with Cuba, saying he knew "how difficult it [was] to accomplish a revolution." Khrushchev continued, "If assurances were given by the President and the government of the United States that the USA itself would not participate in an attack on Cuba and would restrain others from actions of this sort, if you would recall your fleet, this would immediately change everything." Khrushchev closed his message with one of the letter's most striking images. Suggesting that he and Kennedy should show "statesmanlike wisdom," Khrushchev warned:

> Mr. President, we and you ought not now to pull on the ends of the rope in which you have tied the knots of war, because the more the two of us pull, the tighter this knot will be tied. And a moment may come when that knot will be tied so tight that even he who tied will not have the strength to untie it, and then it will be necessary to cut that knot.[9]

The ExCom Reacts to the Message

At 10:00 P.M. that evening, the ExCom met to discuss the letter and the proposal brought to them by John Scali. It appeared that the situation was getting better. Robert Kennedy had a "slight feeling of optimism" over the fact that Khrushchev did not want a military conflict.[10]

The president also felt some relief. Still, he was aware that, while the messages were encouraging, they were not a clear enough basis to end the crisis. He decided to analyze the letter more closely and respond to it the next day.

As the ExCom retired for the evening, Robert Kennedy made a late-night trip to the Soviet Embassy to see Ambassador Dobrynin. The president had sent him there, without telling the rest of the ExCom, to get a better understanding of how serious the Soviets were about the proposals hinted at that day.

Dobrynin's biggest concerns were the missiles in Turkey and getting a promise from the United States never to invade Cuba. By the end of their meeting, Robert Kennedy assured Dobrynin that the United States government was willing to discuss both issues "in a positive way."[11]

As Friday night came to an end, it seemed that the Cuban Missile Crisis would end through a diplomatic solution. Little did the ExCom know that it would face the biggest challenges of the crisis the next day.

The Attack on Major Anderson's Plane

Saturday morning, October 27, began horribly in Havana. Cuba was being pummeled by a tropical storm that threatened communication systems. General Issa Pliyev, commander of the Soviet forces in Cuba, was certain the United States would attack sometime over the weekend. While the Soviets had given him specific orders not to use nuclear weapons without an order from Moscow, Pliyev was authorized to use other forces to defend Cuba. Both the Cubans and the Soviets defending the island were extremely nervous. That morning, Pliyev had left two lieutenant generals in his command with specific orders not to use force without his authorization.

It was in these conditions that Major Rudolph Anderson flew his U-2 plane over Cuba. The U-2 was viewed as an immediate threat to the Soviets in Cuba. Any information that it gathered could be used to plan an attack later. The lieutenant generals were unable to reach Pliyev on the phone. So they acted on their own.

They ordered the firing of the SAM that shot down the U-2, killing Major Anderson.[12]

Another Peculiar Message

At about the same time Anderson's plane was shot down, the ExCom was working on a response to Khrushchev's letter. It was about 10:00 A.M. They were not very far into their discussion when they were interrupted by news that a second Khrushchev letter was coming. This one was very different from the first. It was a public letter being read over Radio Moscow. The president read from the news bulletin, "Premier Khrushchev told President Kennedy yesterday he would withdraw offensive weapons from Cuba if the United States withdrew rockets from Turkey."[13]

The president and the ExCom were confused. Khrushchev had said nothing about United States missiles in Turkey in his previous letter. Except for Robert Kennedy's meeting with Dobrynin (which most of the ExCom did not know about), discussions with the Soviets had centered on exchanging a noninvasion promise for the dismantling of missiles in Cuba. Most of the ExCom believed that the second letter did not come from Khrushchev, but rather from military leaders in the Kremlin who were influencing Khrushchev's handling of the crisis. In fact, it was Khrushchev who, after reconsidering his position in the crisis since his last letter, wanted the United States to pay a higher price to get rid of the missiles in Cuba.[14]

SOURCE DOCUMENT

... HOW ARE WE, THE SOVIET UNION, OUR GOVERNMENT, TO ASSESS YOUR ACTIONS WHICH ARE EXPRESSED IN THE FACT THAT YOU HAVE SURROUNDED THE SOVIET UNION WITH MILITARY BASES; SURROUNDED OUR ALLIES WITH MILITARY BASES; PLACED MILITARY BASES LITERALLY AROUND OUR COUNTRY; AND STATIONED YOUR MISSILE ARMAMENTS THERE? ... YOUR MISSILES ARE LOCATED IN BRITAIN, ARE LOCATED IN ITALY AND ARE AIMED AGAINST US. YOUR MISSILES ARE LOCATED IN TURKEY.

YOU ARE DISTURBED OVER CUBA. YOU SAY THIS DISTURBS YOU BECAUSE IT [CUBA] IS 90 MILES BY SEA FROM THE COAST OF THE UNITED STATES OF AMERICA. BUT TURKEY ADJOINS US.[15]

Soviet leader Nikita Khrushchev made this address, explaining why the Soviet Union felt justified in placing missiles in Cuba.

The second letter put ExCom discussions into a tailspin. No response to either letter had yet been drafted when the group adjourned just before noon. When the ExCom met again at about 4:00 P.M., it was interrupted once again. This time, it was the news about the death of Major Anderson.

A variety of suggestions came from the ExCom. McCone wanted the president to issue a strongly worded statement to Khrushchev, protesting the shooting. He also advocated an air strike as early as Monday morning. In keeping with President Kennedy's standing order to strike any SAM site that shot down a United States plane, F-100s—bombers that could fly at the speed of sound—had begun preparing for launch that morning. The president ordered them to stay. Despite protests from the military, his own feelings about the death of a defenseless American pilot, and the uncertainty of the Soviets' intentions, President Kennedy concentrated on the goal of peacefully ending the crisis.

ExCom discussions returned to Khrushchev's two letters. Ted Sorensen and Robert Kennedy suggested that they respond to the first letter, which they were certain came directly from the Soviet chairman, and ignore the second letter. The United States government would spell out its terms to settle the crisis, avoiding the topic of the missiles in Turkey. Then, Robert Kennedy would meet with Anatoly Dobrynin to discuss the United States' response. They would also discuss a few items, including the first American casualty, which were not part of the United States' response. Dean Rusk coached Robert Kennedy on exactly what to say to the Soviet ambassador.

Robert Kennedy and Dobrynin Meet Again

Dobrynin met the attorney general at about 7:45 P.M. "There is now strong pressure on the president to give an order to respond with fire if fired upon," said Robert Kennedy. "If we start to fire in response—a chain reaction will quickly start that will be very hard to stop."[16]

Kennedy reviewed the points made in the president's reply to Khrushchev. Most important was the removal of the Cuban missiles. Once this was done, the president would end the quarantine and promise that the United States would never invade Cuba.

"And what about Turkey?" Dobrynin asked.[17] Kennedy told the Soviet ambassador that, if American missiles in Turkey were the only issue keeping the Soviet Union from making this agreement, then the president would be willing to remove them.[18] However, it could not happen for another four to five months and it had to be done in secret. It was important to the United States government that neither the Soviet Union, nor any other nation, perceive the agreement as some kind of "swap." That would give the impression that the United States could not stand up to the Soviets, or worse, that it was a nation that would abandon its allies. If the Soviets failed to maintain secrecy, the whole offer would be null and void.

As their meeting ended, Robert Kennedy tried to impress the need for a quick answer upon Dobrynin. He wrote about the meeting in a memo to Dean Rusk:

> [I told Dobrynin] He should understand that if they did not remove those bases then we would remove them. His country might take retaliatory action but he should understand that before this was over, while there might be dead Americans there would also be dead Russians.[19]

DEAR MR. CHAIRMAN,

I HAVE READ YOUR LETTER OF OCTOBER 26TH WITH GREAT CARE AND WELCOMED THE STATEMENT OF YOUR DESIRE TO SEEK A PROMPT SOLUTION TO THE PROBLEM. . . . BUT THE FIRST INGREDIENT, LET ME EMPHASIZE, IS THE CESSATION OF WORK ON MISSILE SITES IN CUBA AND MEASURES TO RENDER SUCH WEAPONS INOPERABLE, UNDER EFFECTIVE INTERNATIONAL GUARANTEES. THE CONTINUATION OF THIS THREAT, OR A PROLONGING OF THIS DISCUSSION CONCERNING CUBA BY LINKING THESE PROBLEMS TO BROADER QUESTIONS OF EUROPEAN AND WORLD SECURITIES, WOULD SURELY LEAD TO AN INTENSIFICATION OF THE CUBAN CRISIS AND A GRAVE RISK TO THE PEACE OF THE WORLD. FOR THIS REASON I HOPE WE CAN QUICKLY AGREE ALONG THE LINES OUTLINED IN THIS LETTER AND IN YOUR LETTER OF OCTOBER 26TH.

SINCERELY,
JOHN F. KENNEDY [20]

President Kennedy wrote this response to Khrushchev's letter of October 26, 1962, outlining his ideas about how the crisis could be resolved.

The End of the Crisis

When he returned to the White House, Robert Kennedy felt that the chance of getting a quick agreement from the Soviets was slim. The situation seemed to be deteriorating. He doubted the Soviets would agree to dismantle their missiles without the United States' publicly removing its missiles in Turkey.

At that evening's ExCom meeting, the discussion was dominated by the issue of what to do about a Soviet tanker, the *Grozny*, which was approaching the line of interdiction. Plans were made for a U-2 flight to go over Cuba, accompanied by fighter planes, in the morning. That alone could escalate into a conflict with the Soviets. Any hope for ending the crisis depended on Khrushchev's actions.

When the ExCom broke up for the day, the mood was grim. Some members stayed in their offices through the night to keep themselves busy. They knew they would not get much sleep if they went home. President Kennedy and his advisor Dave Powers watched the film *Roman Holiday,* starring Audrey Hepburn and Gregory Peck, to keep their minds at ease. Everyone tried to keep his mind off the awful possibility that had been articulated by Robert McNamara. He had said, "It was a perfectly beautiful night. . . . I walked out of the president's Oval Office and as I walked out I thought I might never live to see another Saturday night."[21]

"Robert Kennedy looked exhausted," Dobrynin reported to Khrushchev. "One could see . . . that he had not slept for days." Dobrynin's account of Robert Kennedy's behavior during the Saturday night meeting is very different from Kennedy's account. "I haven't seen my children for days now," said Kennedy, who looked like he was about to cry, according to Dobrynin. "And the president hasn't seen his either. We're spending all day and night at the White House."[22]

When Dobrynin's report reached Khrushchev, the Soviet leader was in the middle of a special meeting with the Presidium and some members of the Communist party's Central Committee. The chairman, having only President Kennedy's latest letter in hand, was trying to convince his government to dismantle the Cuban missiles in exchange for a noninvasion pledge. The missiles in Turkey would have to be given up in the interest of keeping peace. Khrushchev was acting on the fear that the American military was pressuring the president to invade.

Suddenly, Oleg Troyanovsky, an assistant to Khrushchev, burst into the room with Dobrynin's report. The United States would dismantle their missiles in Turkey if an agreement could be reached that very day. Khrushchev wasted no time in dispatching the following message: "I have received your message of October 27. . . . the Soviet Government . . . has given a new order to dismantle the arms which you described as offensive, and to crate and return them to the Soviet Union."[23] The message would be immediately broadcast over Radio Moscow, which would announce to the world that the Cuban Missile Crisis was over.

The news about the Soviets' decision reached Washington at 9:00 A.M. on Sunday, October 28. It made the ExCom ecstatic. All the military preparations would not be necessary. The diplomacy between Robert Kennedy and Anatoly Dobrynin seemed to have worked. As one ExCom member, McGeorge

Bundy, put it, "everyone knew who were the hawks and who were the doves, but . . . today was the doves' day."[24] What he meant was that those who wanted to end the crisis through cautious and peaceful action had been proven right. A diplomatic solution had been found. The crisis was over.

The American public reacted to the news in different ways. For the most part, they simply resumed their normal lives. The news of the end of the crisis first became public on Sunday morning, October 28. Many people missed the first bulletins because they were in church. In Florida, many people went to the beach for the first time in a week.[25] In Washington, D.C., television sets were tuned in to that afternoon's football game between the Washington Redskins and the New York Giants.[26] Overall, the end of the crisis brought a huge sense of relief to the American people.

·10·

AFTERMATH

Relations between the two superpowers returned to normal over the next few months. On November 20, 1962, President Kennedy announced that Soviet ships could be seen leaving Cuba with their dangerous cargoes. The naval quarantine in the Caribbean Sea was lifted the next day, and the Jupiter missiles in Turkey were dismantled by the end of April 1963.

The promise never to invade Cuba, however, was nullified when Castro refused to allow the United Nations to observe the withdrawal of the missiles.[1] However, no American president since the crisis has tried to invade Cuba. Even Kennedy's Operation Mongoose was officially terminated shortly after the Cuban Missile Crisis.

Kennedy, Khrushchev, and Castro After the Crisis

Ironically, the experience of the Cuban Missile Crisis had some positive effects on the Kennedy presidency. The withdrawal of the Soviet missiles gave many people the impression that the president had succeeded in getting the Soviets to back down. Kennedy enjoyed a greater reputation as a statesman. The Cuban Missile

President Kennedy, seen here making a speech in Berlin, Germany, considered the Cuban Missile Crisis one of the biggest successes of his career.

Crisis was perhaps the finest moment of John F. Kennedy's very brief term in office. In November 1963, President Kennedy was assassinated while on a campaign trip in Dallas, Texas.

Nikita Khrushchev's political career, on the other hand, was negatively affected by the crisis. The quiet withdrawal of American missiles from Turkey, as well as Castro's feeling that the Soviet Union had abandoned Cuba, hurt Khrushchev politically. When he returned home from a vacation on October 14, 1964, Khrushchev was quickly brought to a meeting of the Central Committee. Its proceedings took away all his government authority. Among the charges against him were his "reckless" handling of relations with Fidel Castro and a senseless nuclear gamble with the United States. The seventy-year-old leader was ousted from power and replaced with the much younger Leonid Brezhnev. Although Khrushchev was confined to a special residence outside Moscow, he was allowed to have visitors. During this time, Khrushchev wrote two books about his memories of helping to establish and leading the Soviet Union. The books were smuggled out and published in the United States. Nikita Khrushchev died on September 11, 1971.

The most enduring leader of the Cuban Missile Crisis, Fidel Castro, probably welcomed its end the least. He lost the protection of Soviet missiles in exchange for a noninvasion promise from John Kennedy, the man behind the Bay of Pigs invasion and numerous attempts on Castro's life. Feeling that

Khrushchev had betrayed him, Castro temporarily broke off relations with the Soviet Union. He refused to allow United Nations weapons inspectors to verify the removal of the missiles. He also threatened to attack the United States naval base at Guantanamo Bay. On October 29, 1962, Soviet Ambassador Anastas Mikoyan, who was a key figure in forming the Soviet-Cuban alliance, was sent to Cuba to reassure Castro, who eventually re-allied himself with the Soviet Union. Castro remains in power to this day.

Nuclear Disarmament

The most important part of the legacy of the Cuban Missile Crisis was its effect on nuclear disarmament. The experience taught the superpowers—and the world—that the arms race and brinkmanship were dangerous games. Soon after the crisis ended, Kennedy and Khrushchev signed the 1963 Nuclear Test Ban Treaty. In it, both nations promised not to test nuclear weapons in the atmosphere.

In the 1970s, Cold War rivalry eased into a period of détente, or relaxing of tensions. This allowed the superpowers to hold the Strategic Arms Limitation Talks (SALT). These were attempts to limit the number of nuclear weapons each nation would build. However, the most significant disarmament agreement was the Intermediate Range Nuclear Forces Treaty, or INF Treaty, signed by President Ronald Reagan and Soviet General Secretary Mikhail Gorbachev in 1987. Both nations agreed to disable two classes of weapons

THE STATES CONCLUDING THIS TREATY, . . .

BELIEVING THAT THE PROLIFERATION OF NUCLEAR WEAPONS WOULD SERIOUSLY ENHANCE THE DANGER OF NUCLEAR WAR . . .

HAVE AGREED AS FOLLOWS:

ARTICLE I
EACH NUCLEAR-WEAPON STATE PARTY TO THE TREATY UNDERTAKES NOT TO TRANSFER TO ANY RECIPIENT WHAT-SOEVER NUCLEAR WEAPONS OR OTHER NUCLEAR EXPLOSIVE DEVICES OR CONTROL OVER SUCH WEAPONS OR EXPLOSIVE DEVICES DIRECTLY, OR INDIRECTLY; AND NOT IN ANY WAY TO ASSIST, ENCOURAGE, OR INDUCE ANY NON-NUCLEAR-WEAPON STATE TO MANUFACTURE OR OTHERWISE ACQUIRE NUCLEAR WEAPONS OR OTHER NUCLEAR EXPLOSIVE DEVICES, OR CONTROL OVER SUCH WEAPONS OR EXPLOSIVE DEVICES.[2]

Many nations, including the United States and Soviet Union, signed the 1968 Nuclear Non-Proliferation Treaty, aimed at limiting the number of countries that had nuclear weapons.

systems and to allow for on-site military inspections on each other's territory.

The INF Treaty foreshadowed an even greater event between the United States and the Soviet Union. In the late 1980s, Mikhail Gorbachev began to ease his nation's grip on Eastern Europe. Communism collapsed in those countries, and eventually, in the rest of the Soviet Union as well. Without the support of the Soviet Union, East Germany's Communist government disbanded. In November 1989, overjoyed citizens from both sides of Berlin tore down the Berlin Wall. The Cold War was coming to an end.

Unfortunately, the end of the Cold War did not rid the world of the dangers of nuclear weapons. Since the days of the Cuban Missile Crisis, many more nations have acquired atomic weapons. Any conflict involving these nations has the possibility of returning the world to the same danger faced in October 1962.

Recent land disputes between India and Pakistan have involved leaders threatening nuclear attack. Such a situation echoes the feelings that John F. Kennedy expressed to a friend early in the Cuban Missile Crisis, that "the existence of nuclear arms made a secure and rational world impossible."[3] As long as nuclear weapons exist, the world's only safeguard is leaders who have the same fear of war as John F. Kennedy and Nikita Khrushchev.

★ TIMELINE ★

1823—Monroe Doctrine is issued, closing the Western Hemisphere to further European colonization.

1898—The Spanish-American War is fought; Cuba becomes independent from Spain.

1903—Platt Amendment makes Cuba protectorate of the United States.

1904—The Roosevelt Corollary to the Monroe Doctrine is announced.

1917—The Soviet Union is established.

1933—Good Neighbor Policy begins.

1945—*May 7*: Nazi Germany surrenders to the Allies, ending World War II in Europe.
August: Atomic bombs are dropped on Japan.
September 2: Japan surrenders, ending World War II.

1948—Organization of American States (OAS) formed.

1949—The Soviet Union detonates an atomic bomb.

1952—Fulgencio Batista becomes dictator of Cuba.

1953—Fidel Castro attempts to overthrow Batista; The M-26-7 movement begins.

1959—Fidel Castro takes over the Cuban government.

1960—*February*: Cuba and the Soviet Union make a trade agreement.
March 17: President Eisenhower approves a CIA plan to remove Castro from power.

1961—*January 10*: An article describing a plan to invade Cuba forces Eisenhower to delay.
January 20: John F. Kennedy is inaugurated.
April 17: Bay of Pigs invasion fails.

June: Kennedy and Soviet leader Nikita Khrushchev meet, to discuss problems in Berlin.

August 13: Berlin Wall is built.

1962—*May–June*: Cuba receives non-nuclear military weapons from the Soviet Union.

August 22: CIA reports the Soviet military buildup to President Kennedy.

August 29: American U-2 spy planes discover Soviet surface-to-air missiles in Cuba; Kennedy aide Ted Sorensen meets with Ambassador Anatoly Dobrynin; Dobrynin explains that the weapons are strictly defensive.

September 4: President Kennedy warns that "the gravest of issues would arise" if any offensive weapons were found in Cuba.

October 14: The Cuban Missile Crisis begins after the National Photographic Interpretation Center (NPIC) examines film from U-2 flights and confirms that medium-range ballistic missiles (MRBMs) are in Cuba; No evidence of nuclear warheads is found.

October 16: President Kennedy is informed about the missiles in Cuba; The Executive Committee (ExCom) meets for the first time; A possible air strike against Cuba is scheduled for October 20; Khrushchev meets with United States Ambassador Foy Kohler in Moscow, giving a message that tells President Kennedy that no surface-to-surface missiles are in Cuba.

October 18: President Kennedy, Secretary of State Dean Rusk, and Ambassador Llewellyn Thompson meet with Soviet Foreign Minister Andrei Gromyko and Ambassador Dobrynin; Gromyko says that the Soviet Union has put only defensive weapons in Cuba.

October 19: President Kennedy goes on a campaign trip to Chicago; ExCom considers an air strike or a naval blockade of Cuba.

October 20: CIA reports that eight MRBMs could be fired on the United States that very day; Still, no nuclear warheads have been found on the island; President Kennedy decides to use a naval blockade, which he calls a quarantine, around Cuba.

October 22: President Kennedy addresses the nation, informing the public about the missiles in Cuba and the quarantine.

October 23: More U-2 flights are ordered over Cuba; Khrushchev protests the quarantine as a violation of international law; The OAS votes in favor of the quarantine; President Kennedy signs the Proclamation of Interdiction; Nuclear warheads reach Cuba; Robert Kennedy meets secretly with Dobrynin.

October 24: Nuclear warheads are mounted onto the MRBMs in Cuba; A bartender overhears two journalists mention an American invasion of Cuba and informs Aleksandr Feklisov; Khrushchev meets with American businessman William Knox in Moscow, giving Knox a message in which he admits placing missiles in Cuba and suggests a meeting to end the crisis; Soviet oil tanker *Bucharest* approaches the quarantine, testing the naval line for the first time.

October 25: Khrushchev decides to remove the missiles from Cuba; Journalist Walter Lippmann suggests that the United States remove its missiles from Turkey in exchange for the Soviets' removing their missiles from Cuba; Adlai Stevenson confronts Soviet Ambassador Valerian Zorin at the United Nations.

October 26: Press Secretary Pierre Salinger reports that construction of the Soviet missile sites in Cuba has accelerated; Aleksandr Feklisov meets with American journalist John Scali and talks about a three-point plan to end the crisis; Scali informs the State Department of the meeting; A strange message from Khrushchev is received by the White House; ExCom meets to discuss the Feklisov-Scali meeting and the Khrushchev letter; Robert Kennedy secretly meets with Dobrynin and says the United States would consider removing its missiles from Turkey.

October 27: Major Rudolph Anderson is killed when his U-2 is shot down in Cuba; ExCom receives a second message from Khrushchev saying the United States must withdraw its missiles from Turkey if it hopes to resolve the crisis; Robert Kennedy secretly meets with Dobrynin to demand that the Soviet Union agree to remove its missiles from Cuba by the following day; Kennedy also says he is authorized to promise that missiles would be withdrawn from Turkey, but that it must be kept secret.

October 28: Khrushchev agrees to remove the missiles from Cuba.

November 20: President Kennedy reports that Soviet ships have been seen carrying missiles away from Cuba.

★ Chapter Notes ★

Chapter 1. What Was Everyone So Afraid of?

1. David Detzer, *The Brink* (New York: Thomas Y. Crowell Publishers, 1979), p. 248.

2. Robert Kennedy, *Thirteen Days: A Memoir of the Cuban Missile Crisis* (New York: Norton, 1969), p. 105.

3. Ibid., p. 98.

4. Ibid., p. 31.

5. Detzer, p. 248.

6. Norman H. Finkelstein, *Thirteen Days/Ninety Miles: The Cuban Missile Crisis* (New York: Julian Messner, 1994), p. 93.

7. *Doomsday: On The Brink*, The Learning Channel, 1998.

8. Ibid.

9. Ernest R. May and Philip D. Zelikow, eds., *The Kennedy Tapes: Inside the White House During the Cuban Missile Crisis* (Cambridge, Mass.: The Belknap Press of Harvard University Press, 1997), p. 519.

10. Detzer, p. 248.

11. Kennedy, p. l08.

12. *Dobrynin's Cable to the Soviet Foreign Ministry,* October 27, 1962, Cold War International History Project.

13. Kennedy, p. 109.

Chapter 2. The Cold War

1. Alexander Leighton. "That Day at Hiroshima," *Atlantic Monthly*, October 1946, p. 87.

2. Ibid.

3. Ibid., pp. 87–88.

4. Ibid., p. 88.

5. Kevin Rafferty, Jayne Loader, and Pierce Rafferty, *The Atomic Cafe* (New York: First Run Features, 1982).

6. Ibid.

Chapter 3. How Did Cuba Get in the Middle?

1. *The Cold War*, television documentary, CNN, 1998.

2. Henry Steele Commager, ed., *Documents of American History*, 6th ed. (New York: Appleton-Century-Crofts, Inc., 1958), vol. 1, pp. 236–237.

3. Annual Message from President Theodore Roosevelt to the U.S. Congress, December 3, 1901, *Foreign Relations of the United States* (FRUS) 1901, pp. ix, xxxvi.

4. Treaty of Relations between the United States and Cuba, signed at Havana, May 22, 1903.

5. Address by President Theodore Roosevelt in Chicago, April 2, 1903, quoted in James W. Gantenbein, ed., *The Evolution of Our Latin-American Policy: A Documentary Record* (New York: Octagon Books, 1971), p. 361.

6. Treaty of Relations between the United States and Cuba, signed in Washington, D.C., May 29, 1934.

7. Thomas G. Paterson, *Contesting Castro: The United States and the Triumph of the Cuban Revolution* (New York: Oxford University Press, 1994), p. 59.

8. Ibid., p. 35.

9. Ibid., p. 36.

10. Ibid., p. 35.

11. Ibid., p. 40.

12. Ibid., p. 51.

13. Dwight D. Eisenhower, *Waging Peace 1956–1961* (Garden City, N.Y.: Doubleday & Co., 1965), p. 520.

14. Paterson, p. 255.

15. Paul Halsall, "Fidel Castro: On the Export of Revolution," *Modern History Sourcebook*, July 1998, <http://www.fordham.edu/halsall/mod/castro-revolution.html> (June 2, 2000).

16. *The 20th Century: Fidel Castro*, television documentary, CBS News Archives.

17. Aleksandr Fursenko and Timothy Naftali, *"One Hell of a Gamble": Khrushchev, Castro & Kennedy, 1958–1964* (New York: W. W. Norton & Company, 1997), p. 39.

Chapter 4. Soviet Missiles in Cuba

1. Robert E. Quirk, *Fidel Castro* (New York: W. W. Norton & Company, 1993), p. 349.

2. Aleksandr Fursenko and Timothy Naftali, *"One Hell of a Gamble": Khrushchev, Castro & Kennedy, 1958–1964* (New York: W. W. Norton & Company, 1997), p. 83.

3. JFK campaign speech, Tampa, Florida, October 18, 1960, quoted in Fursenko and Naftali, p. 83.

4. Stephen E. Ambrose, *Eisenhower, Volume Two, The President* (New York: Simon & Schuster, 1984), p. 527.

5. Dwight D. Eisenhower, *Waging Peace 1956–1961* (Garden City, N.Y.: Doubleday & Company, Inc., 1965), p. 614.

6. Ernest R. May and Philip D. Zelikow, eds., *The Kennedy Tapes: Inside the White House During the Cuban Missile Crisis* (Cambridge, Mass.: The Belknap Press of Harvard University Press, 1997), p. 30.

7. *The Cuban Missile Crisis*, television documentary, The History Channel.

8. Ibid.

9. Arthur M. Schlesinger, Jr., *A Thousand Days* (New York: Fawcett Premier, 1965), p. 348.

10. Fursenko and Naftali, p. 178.

11. Raymond L. Garthoff, *Reflections on the Cuban Missile Crisis* (Washington, D.C.: The Brookings Institution, 1989), p. 10.

Chapter 5. Finding out About the Missiles

1. Dino A. Brugioni, *Eyeball to Eyeball: The Inside Story of the Cuban Missile Crisis* (New York: Random House, 1990), p. 111.

2. Ibid.

3. Aleksandr Fursenko and Timothy Naftali, *"One Hell of a Gamble": Khrushchev, Castro & Kennedy, 1958–1964* (New York: W. W. Norton & Co., 1997), p. 205.

4. Ibid., p. 199.

5. Norman H. Finkelstein, *Thirteen Days/Ninety Miles: The Cuban Missile Crisis* (New York: Simon & Schuster, 1994), p. 30.

6. Fursenko and Naftali, p. 204.

7. Finkelstein, p. 31.

8. Roy Medvedev, *Khrushchev* (Garden City, N.Y.: Anchor Press/Doubleday, 1983), p. 185.

9. Fursenko and Naftali, p. 206.

10. Arthur J. Olsen, "Kennedy Pledges Any Steps to Bar Cuban Aggression," *The New York Times*, September 5, 1962, p. 1.

11. Ibid.

12. Medvedev, p. 186.

13. Ibid., p. 187.

14. Ernest R. May and Philip D. Zelikow, eds., *The Kennedy Tapes: Inside the White House During the Cuban Missile Crisis* (Cambridge, Mass.: The Belknap Press of Harvard University Press, 1997), p. 46.

Chapter 6. Keeping up Appearances

1. Arthur M. Schlesinger, Jr., *A Thousand Days: John F. Kennedy in the White House* (New York: Fawcett Premier Books, 1965), p. 734.

2. Ernest R. May and Philip D. Zelikow, eds., *The Kennedy Tapes: Inside the White House During the Cuban Missile Crisis* (Cambridge, Mass.: The Belknap Press of Harvard University Press, 1997), pp. 47–49.

3. Robert Kennedy, *Thirteen Days: A Memoir of the Cuban Missile Crisis* (New York: Norton, 1969), pp. 23–24.

4. Aleksandr Fursenko and Timothy Naftali, *"One Hell of a Gamble": Khrushchev, Castro & Kennedy, 1958–1964* (New York: W. W. Norton & Co., 1997), p. 51.

5. Ibid., p. 224.

6. Dino A. Brugioni, *Eyeball to Eyeball: The Inside Story of the Cuban Missile Crisis* (New York: Random House, 1990), p. 232.

7. Ibid.

8. May and Zelikow, p. 55.

9. Fursenko and Naftali, pp. 226–227.

10. Ibid., p. 229.

11. Norman H. Finkelstein, *Thirteen Days/Ninety Miles: The Cuban Missile Crisis* (New York: Simon & Schuster, 1994), p. 53.

12. Fursenko and Naftali, p. 232.

13. Ibid., p. 229.

14. Ibid., p. 230.

15. Ibid.

16. Ibid., p. 231.

17. Brugioni, p. 286.

18. Ibid., pp. 286–287.

19. Ibid.

20. Fursenko and Naftali, p. 232.

Chapter 7. Making Decisions and Going Public

1. Arthur M. Schlesinger, *A Thousand Days: John F. Kennedy in the White House* (New York: Fawcett Premier, 1965), p. 738.

2. Aleksandr Fursenko and Timothy Naftali, *"One Hell of a Gamble": Khrushchev, Castro & Kennedy, 1958–1964* (New York: W. W. Norton & Company, 1997), p. 235.

3. Ibid.

4. Ibid.

5. Ernest R. May and Philip D. Zelikow, eds., *The Kennedy Tapes: Inside the White House During the Cuban Missile Crisis* (Cambridge, Mass.: The Belknap Press of Harvard University Press, 1997), pp. 258–259.

6. Dino A. Brugioni, *Eyeball to Eyeball: The Inside Story of the Cuban Missile Crisis* (New York: Random House, 1990), pp. 366–368.

7. May and Zelikow, p. 275.

8. Ibid., p. 269.

9. Brugioni, p. 279.

10. May and Zelikow, p. 275.

11. Fursenko and Naftali, p. 237.

12. Ibid., p. 241.

13. Historical Text Archive, "JFK Address to the Nation on The Cuban Missile Crisis," *The Cuban Missile Crisis*, n.d., <http://www.multied.com/JFKCuba.txt> (June 1, 2000).

14. Ibid.

15. Ibid.

16. Ibid.

17. Ibid.

18. Quoted in Fursenko and Naftali, pp. 281–282.

19. Fursenko and Naftali, p. 247.

Chapter 8. Brinkmanship

1. Arthur M. Schlesinger, Jr., *A Thousand Days* (New York: Fawcett Premier, 1965), p. 749.

2. Amica Palmer, "Phone Interview with my mother Tami Gold," *Collective Memories of the Cuban Missile Crisis*, n.d., <http://www.stg.brown.edu/projects/projects.old/classes/mc166k/ap_3.19.html> (June 2, 2000).

3. Ernest R. May and Philip D. Zelikow, eds., *The Kennedy Tapes: Inside the White House During the Cuban Missile Crisis* (Cambridge, Mass.: The Belknap Press of Harvard University Press, 1997), pp. 390–391.

4. Ibid., p. 321.

5. Aleksandr Fursenko and Timothy Naftali, *"One Hell of a Gamble": Khrushchev, Castro & Kennedy, 1958–1964* (New York: W. W. Norton & Co., 1997), p. 248.

6. Dino A. Brugioni, *Eyeball to Eyeball: The Inside Story of the Cuban Missile Crisis* (New York: Random House, 1990), pp. 379–380.

7. May and Zelikow, p. 322.

8. Fursenko and Naftali, p. 255.

9. Ibid., p. 252.

10. Ibid., p. 253.

11. Norman H. Finkelstein, *Thirteen Days/Ninety Miles: The Cuban Missile Crisis* (New York: Simon & Schuster, 1994), p. 77.

12. Fursenko and Naftali, p. 256.

13. Ibid., p. 262.

14. May and Zelikow, p. 421.

15. Fursenko and Naftali, p. 259.

16. Nikita Khrushchev, *Khrushchev Remembers,* trans. and ed. Strobe Talbot (Boston: Little, Brown & Company, 1970), p. 497.

17. Fursenko and Naftali, pp. 236–237.

18. Brugioni, p. 426.

19. Ibid., p. 427.

20. Ibid.

21. Ibid.

22. Ibid., p. 429.

Chapter 9. The Most Dangerous Days of the Cold War

1. Ernest R. May and Philip D. Zelikow, eds., *The Kennedy Tapes: Inside the White House During the Cuban Missile Crisis* (Cambridge, Mass.: The Belknap Press of Harvard University Press, 1997), p. 440.

2. Ibid., pp. 472–473.

3. Ibid., p. 479.

4. Aleksandr Fursenko and Timothy Naftali, *"One Hell of a Gamble": Khrushchev, Castro & Kennedy, 1958–1964* (New York: W. W. Norton & Co., 1997), p. 265.

5. Norman H. Finkelstein, *Thirteen Days/Ninety Miles: The Cuban Missile Crisis* (New York: Simon & Schuster, 1994), p. 86.

6. Ibid.

7. Letter from Khrushchev to President Kennedy of October 26, 1962, as printed in May and Zelikow, pp. 485–486.

8. Ibid., p. 486.

9. Ibid., p. 490.

10. Robert F. Kennedy, *Thirteen Days: A Memoir of the Cuban Missile Crisis* (New York: Norton, 1969), p. 90.

11. Finkelstein, p. 89.

12. Fursenko and Naftali, p. 277.

13. May and Zelikow, p. 494.

14. Fursenko and Naftali, p. 280.

15. David Colbert, ed., *Eyewitness to America: 500 Years of America in the Words of Those Who Saw It Happen* (New York: Pantheon Books, 1997), p. 467.

16. Ibid., p. 282.

17. Ibid.

18. Ibid.

19. Robert Kennedy to Dean Rusk, October 30, 1962, quoted in May and Zelikow, pp. 607–608.

20. Andrew Carroll, ed., *Letters of a Nation* (New York: Kodansha International, 1997), pp. 164–165.

21. *The Cold War: Cuba*, Turner Original Productions, 1998.

22. Nikita Khrushchev, *Khrushchev Remembers*, trans. and ed. Strobe Talbot (Boston: Little, Brown & Company, 1970), p. 498.

23. "Khrushchev Message of October 28, 1962," quoted in Fursenko and Naftali, p. 285.

24. Ibid., p. 287.

25. Robert Smith Thompson, *The Missiles of October: The Declassified Story of John F. Kennedy and the Cuban Missile Crisis* (New York: Simon & Schuster, 1992), p. 343.

26. Ibid., p. 344.

Chapter 10. Aftermath

1. Ernest R. May and Philip D. Zelikow, eds., *The Kennedy Tapes: Inside the White House During the Cuban Missile Crisis* (Cambridge, Mass.: The Belknap Press of Harvard University Press, 1997), pp. 665–666.

2. United Nations, "The Treaty on Non-Proliferation of Nuclear Weapons (NPT)," *Treaty on the Non-Proliferation of Nuclear Weapons*, 2000, <http://www.un.org/Depts/dda/WMD/npttext.html> (June 2, 2000).

3. Aleksandr Fursenko and Timothy Naftali, *"One Hell of a Gamble": Khrushchev, Castro & Kennedy, 1958–1964* (New York: W. W. Norton & Co., 1997), p. 236.

★ FURTHER READING ★

Harrison, Barbara G., and Daniel Terris. *A Twilight Struggle: The Life of John Fitzgerald Kennedy.* New York: Lothrop, Lee & Shepard Books, 1992.

Kallen, Stuart A. *The Khrushchev Era.* Minneapolis, Minn.: ABDO Publishing Company, 1992.

Kennedy, Robert. *Thirteen Days: A Memoir of the Cuban Missile Crisis.* New York: Norton, 1969.

Rice, Earle, Jr. *The Cuban Revolution.* San Diego, Calif.: Lucent Books, 1995.

Spies, Karen Bornemann. *John F. Kennedy.* Berkeley Heights, N.J.: Enslow Publishers, Inc., 1999.

Tegnell, Geoffrey, and Thomas Ladenburg. *Revolution & Intervention: U.S.-Cuba Relations in the 20th Century.* Boulder, Colo.: Social Science Education Consortium, Inc., 1992.

★ INTERNET ADDRESSES ★

Collective Memories of the Cuban Missile Crisis. n.d. <http://www.stg.brown.edu/projects.old/classes/mc166k/missile_crisis_34.html>.

Halsall, Paul. "Fidel Castro: On the Export of Revolution." *Modern History Sourcebook.* July 1998. <http://www.fordham.edu/halsall/mod/castro-revolution.html>.

★ INDEX ★